THE OLYMPICS AND ME

Other *I Want to Know About* Books:

A FLIGHT TO THE MOON, *by Col. Alfred M. Worden*
THE UNITED STATES SENATE, *by Senator Charles Percy*
VINCENT PRICE, *by Vincent Price*
ALEX KARRAS, *by Alex Karras*
PETE ROSE, *by Pete Rose*

An *I Want to Know About* Book

THE OLYMPICS AND ME

by Bruce Jenner

with R. Smith Kiliper

CONCEIVED AND PRODUCED
BY WHITEHALL, HADLYME & SMITH, INC.

Doubleday & Company, Inc., Garden City, New York

To my dog Bertha for all her dedicated years of training with me.

Library of Congress Cataloging in Publication Data

Jenner, Bruce, 1949–
The Olympics and me.

(An I want to know about book)
Includes index.
SUMMARY: The 1976 Olympics decathlon winner discusses his life, his Olympic experiences, the decathlon, and his involvement in the Special Olympics.
1. Jenner, Bruce, 1949– —Juvenile literature. 2. Track and field athletes–United States–Biography–Juvenile literature. 3. Olympic games –Juvenile literature. 4. Decathlon–Juvenile literature. [1. Jenner, Bruce, 1949– 2. Track and field athletes. 3. Decathlon]

I. Kiliper, R. Smith, joint author. II. Title.
GV697.J38A36 796.4'2'0924 [B] [92]
ISBN: 0-385-14928-x Trade
0-385-14929-8 Prebound
Library of Congress Catalog Card Number 79–7496

PRINTED IN THE UNITED STATES OF AMERICA
FIRST EDITION

When I was a boy, it seemed that some of the best times of the school day were the assembly programs. They were often joyous links to the world outside the classroom. They were concerned with a world where true-life literature happened, where bridges were built, where dreams could become reality. I never forgot those experiences. When I ultimately became a literary producer, I decided to create the *I Want to Know About* series as a way of putting something back into the educational process. Recognizing how many unanswered questions young people have about the real world, I arranged to bring well-known people into schools and have them join with students in informal sessions where they answer all sorts of questions about their lives, their careers, and their feelings. The results are books that tell all young people about what it is really like to be an astronaut, a senator, a football player, an actor, a baseball player, or a person engaged in any one of countless other human pursuits. It is my hope that, whether you are in school or out, this series of books will appeal to your curiosity and, in so doing, will cause you to become more excited about the world and the opportunities around you.

R. Smith Kiliper
President, Whitehall, Hadlyme & Smith, Inc.

I would like to express my sincere thanks to Mr. Allen Wallach for arranging the session with the children of the Paige School in Los Angeles, as well as to Mrs. Ann Olmstead, the principal, and to all of the youngsters of the Paige School for their co-operation with me in the preparation of this book. My special thanks to the following students for asking me such great questions. They are:

Susie Boctor
Eldren Copez
Jerald Crucillo
Joyce Crucillo
Jason Farber
Steven Hall
Charles Harvey
David Holland
James Holland
Darren Hortel
Monica Lee
Tony Lewis
Stefano Marrero
Julie Perry
Andrea Schultz
Yvette Tijunait

Bruce Jenner

Contents

1. The Olympics and the Decathlon

The first Olympic Games were held in Ancient Greece. It happened a long time ago—776 B.C.—as far as we know. And the first Olympics weren't much. The only event was a 200-yard footrace near the city of Olympia, in southwestern Greece.

The Games were held every four years. And gradually, as event after event was added, they became more and more complicated. The Games continued for over a thousand years. But only men could compete. Then, in A.D. 394, the Games were banned because they had become too professional. You see, the original idea was to have no one in the Games who was not an amateur.

More than a thousand years went by. Then, in 1896, the first modern Olympic Games were held in Athens, Greece. These Games were the idea of a Frenchman, though—not a Greek. His name was Baron Pierre de Coubertin. And his idea was to promote greater interest in education and culture and to encourage international understanding. He thought that he could do that by inviting athletes from many countries to compete against each other.

(Photo by Chrystie Jenner)

There were athletes from eight nations in those first modern Olympic Games. Since then, the number of countries has risen to more than one hundred.

Except for the years of World Wars I and II, the Olympics have been held every four years since 1896. More and more events have been added. And since 1924 there have been Winter Olympics, too.

The event that is the most important to me, the decathlon, was added in 1912. Most record books now list the winner of that event, held in Stockholm, Sweden, as the Swedish athlete Hugo Wieslander. But he did not score the most points in the 1912 decathlon.

Jim Thorpe, the superb Native American athlete, outscored Wieslander. Unfortunately, it was later found that Thorpe had played semiprofessional baseball before he went to the Olympics. That lost him his amateur standing and cost him his gold medals for the decathlon and the pentathlon.

It probably was at the Stockholm Olympics that the business of calling the decathlon champion the "world's greatest athlete" began. As I said, Jim Thorpe had won the event. When King Gustaf V of Sweden gave him the gold medal, the King said, "You are the greatest athlete in the world."

It is said that Thorpe replied, "Thanks, King."

Anyway, the title has stuck—the champion decathlete is always called the "world's greatest athlete." Personally, I don't consider myself the "world's greatest athlete." If I am the world's greatest athlete, why can't I hit a golf ball straight? Perhaps nobody deserves that title, anyway.

Does this look like "the world's greatest athlete"? Chrystie and I are definitely not perfect in all sports.
(Michael Alexander, *People*, © 1976 Time Inc.)

But what is the decathlon? Simply put, it is a ten-event competition. Every decathlete participates in all ten events. He gets points for each of his individual performances and the ten point scores are added up. The man with the highest total wins the decathlon.

The running of the decathlon takes two days, and here are the events:

FIRST DAY

100-meter run
Long jump
Shot put
High jump
400-meter run

SECOND DAY

110-meter hurdles
Discus throw
Pole vault
Javelin throw
1,500-meter run

You participate by running against an international scorecard. Everyone in any decathlon runs against the same scorecard. You start out by running the 100-meter as fast as you can. When the race is over, you find out what your time was. Then you find out how many points that time gives you on the scorecard. You might get 800 or 900 points, depending on how fast you ran.

Then you jump as high as you can, throw as far as you can, and so on. You add up all the points for the ten events and you get a total score. Finally, you hope that you have more points than anyone else in the decathlon.

Then there is tennis. I may look a little like Jimmy Connors, but I don't play like him, even though I am also left-handed. (Photo by Don Mazer)

Here's an explanation of that scorecard. It is an abbreviated scoring table, because if we printed the complete one, with all of the possible times and distances and heights, it would run about forty pages.

Notice that if you run the 100-meter in 12 seconds, you get 580 points. Shave just ½ second off your time, and your score goes up 107 points—to 687. Adding just 6 inches to your long jump, from 24 feet to 24 feet 6 inches adds 31 points to your score. And so on.

100-meter Run

Seconds	*Points*
10.0	1,072
10.2	1,014
10.4	959
10.6	905
10.8	853
11.0	804
11.2	756
11.5	687
12.0	580

Long Jump

Feet/inches	*Meters*	*Points*
26/0	7.91	1,001
25/6	7.77	974
25/0	7.62	945
24/6	7.47	915
24/0	7.31	884
23/6	7.16	853
23/0	7.01	822
22/6	6.86	791
22/0	6.71	758

Shot Put

Feet	*Meters*	*Points*
53	16.16	856
52	15.85	839

High Jump

Feet/inches	*Meters*	*Points*
7/3	2.20	1,025
7/0	2.13	966

51	15.54	820	6/10	2.08	925
50	15.24	803	6/8	2.03	882
49	14.93	784	6/6	1.98	840
48	14.63	766	6/4	1.93	796
47	14.32	747	6/2	1.88	751
46	14.02	729	6/0	1.83	707
45	13.72	710	5/10	1.77	652

400-meter Run

Seconds	*Points*
46.0	1,000
46.5	973
47.0	948
47.2	938
47.5	923
47.8	908
48.0	898
48.2	889
48.5	875
48.8	861
49.0	852
50.0	805
51.0	762
52.0	720
53.0	679

110-meter Hurdles

Seconds	*Points*
13.5	1,023
14.0	963
14.2	939
14.4	915
14.6	892
14.8	870
15.0	848
15.5	797
16.0	749

Discus

Feet	*Meters*	*Points*
180	54.86	956
175	53.34	930
170	51.82	904
165	50.29	877
160	48.78	850
155	47.26	820
150	45.72	795
145	44.18	766
140	42.66	737
135	41.14	708
130	39.62	678

Pole Vault

Feet/inches	*Meters*	*Points*
16/5	5.00	1,052
16/0	4.87	1,021
15/9	4.80	1,005
15/6	4.72	986
15/3	4.65	969
15/0	4.57	950
14/9	4.49	930
14/6	4.42	913
14/3	4.34	894
14/0	4.26	874
13/6	4.42	913
13/0	3.96	796

Javelin Throw

Feet	*Meters*	*Points*
250	76.22	948
240	73.16	915
230	70.12	880
220	67.03	845
210	64.02	810
200	60.96	773
190	57.88	735

1,500-meter Run

Minutes: seconds	*Points*
3:50	905
4:00	816
4:05	775
4:10	735
4:15	696
4:20	660
4:25	624
4:30	590

I sometimes think of the decathlon as an event of mediocrity. Not that decathletes are mediocre. Far from it. It's just that if you take one event at a time, none of us is really a world-class athlete at that particular event. It's the over-all ability that makes us different.

Just to show you how good (or how bad) a decathlete's performance would be if he were to compete with a specialist, let's look at my 1976 Olympic performance as compared to the Olympic records for each event. And remember that my decathlon total set a world record.

	My Record	*Olympic Record*
100-meter run	10.94 sec.	9.9 sec. (Hines, U.S.)
Long jump	23 ft. 8¼ in.	29 ft. 2½ in. (Beamon, U.S.)
Shot put	50 ft. 4¼ in.	69 ft. 6 in. (Komar, Pol.)
High jump	6 ft. 8 in.	7 ft. 4½ in. (Wszola, Pol.)
400-meter run	47.5 sec.	43.8 sec. (Evans, U.S.)
110-meter hurdles	14.84 sec.	13.24 sec. (Milburn, U.S.)
Discus throw	164 ft. 1 in.	221 ft. 5.4 in. (Wilkins, U.S.)
Pole vault	15 ft. 9 in.	18 ft. ½ in. (Slusarski, Pol., and Norwig, E. Germ.)

Javelin throw	224 ft. 10 in.	310 ft. 4½ in. (Nemeth, Hung.)
1,500-meter run	4 min. 12.3 sec.	3 min. 34.9 sec. (Keino, Kenya)

You can see that I didn't really come too close in any of those events. But if any of those Olympic record holders were to compete in the decathlon, they would undoubtedly lose. They might, and probably would, win their own special event. But they would probably be far down on the list in the other nine.

The winner of the decathlon is the best over-all—not just in one event. You can come in second or third in several events and still have the highest total. For example, I won the 1976 Olympic decathlon, but I still came in second in the 1,500-meter run.

A better example of that would be Rafer Johnson, who won the decathlon in the 1960 Summer Olympic Games in Rome. He came in first in only one event, the shot put. An athlete from China (Taiwan), C. K. Yang, won seven of the other nine. But Johnson was close to Yang in those seven and outdistanced him so much in the discus, shot put, and javelin that he won the Gold Medal.

The decathlon takes a different type of person from the single-event expert. You have to want to excel in a sport that has very little publicity connected with it most of the time. It doesn't compare in glamour with sports such as football, basketball, and baseball. Also, you can't make any money out there in the stadium.

It's an amateur sport and an individual sport. So you get a different type of mental outlook and a different type of personality in a decathlete.

The only time that most people are interested in the sport occurs once every four years. That's at the Olympics, and obviously the interest is extremely high then. But in the years between the Olympic Games, there is almost no publicity or recognition. That eliminates the motivation for a lot of competitors.

The decathlete is not doing his thing because he wants a lot of money or a lot of glory. He will only get those if he wins the Olympic decathlon. Then he seems to be regarded as a national treasure.

Actually, the decathlon has caught on in this country as a non-Olympic sport only in the last few years. But even now it is not seen much in local meets. It is seen in the big relay meets where the games go on for at least two days. This is because no one could run a decathlon in a single day and live to tell about it. That means that you rarely see the decathlon below the level of a state meet.

It used to be that the typical decathlete started out as a quarter-miler, a shot-putter, and a high-jumper. He was pretty good at two or three events while he was in high school, but not outstanding. Then he heard about the decathlon and decided to try it. The result was that he became an athlete who did best in what he did pretty well and tried to hang in there in the other events.

But since the early 1970s there has been a National Collegiate Athletic Association championship decathlon.

That started coaches to look upon their decathletes as a different breed of athlete. They started to think of coaching decathlon specialists, rather than just coaching some men who could do a few things pretty well. It helped the sport a great deal.

Now, in colleges across the country, we have these specialists. All they do in athletics is train for the decathlon. And this interest on the college level is bound to filter down to the high schools.

We have come a long way since the Olympic Games of the Ancient Greeks. Even the awards are different. In the early Greek Olympics, laurel-leaf wreaths were given to the first-place finishers, wild olive-leaf wreaths to runners-up, and palm-leaf wreaths to third-placers.

Today, as everybody knows, the athletes get gold, silver, and bronze medals for first-, second-, and third-place finishes.

The gold medal is actually made of silver coated with about six grams (a little over one fifth of an ounce) of fine gold. The silver medal is made of pure silver, and the bronze medal is pure bronze.

But it isn't a matter of what the medal is worth in dollars and cents. It's the pride that you feel when you win it.

And here is one last wonderful thing about an Olympic medal. When I received my gold medal at

There is nothing like a gold Olympic medal to make you smile. (*Sports Illustrated* Photo by Heinz Kluetmeier)

USA

Montreal, do you know who was the first human being to touch it? I was.

The medals are stamped, ribboned, and boxed without being touched by human hands. And you will notice that when they are awarded, the person hanging the medal around the athlete's neck holds it by the ribbon. So the winner of the medal is the first one to clutch it in his or her hand.

2. Those Were the Days

I was born in Mt. Kisco, New York, on October 28, 1949. Now that's just a few days before Hallowe'en. And to this day there are those people who tell me to take my mask off when I'm not wearing one.

I guess you might say that I was born into an athletic family. For example, my grandfather had run in the Boston Marathon fifteen times. That is a distance of 26 miles 385 yards. Try doing that fifteen different times.

My father, Bill Jenner, was a tree surgeon. He was also an athlete, having competed in the United States Army Olympics in Nuremberg, West Germany, in 1945. He did pretty well, winning a silver medal in the 100-yard dash.

My mother is the disciplinarian of the outfit. But she is a modern woman—a real competitor.

Actually, we were a competitive family. There were my two sisters, my brother, my mother, and my father. We enjoyed doing things together. We went on vacations together. We even competed in water-skiing meets together. The whole family got into it. It seemed

as if every weekend we would take off for another tournament. We went all over New England, New York, and even as far away as Virginia.

It was a fun time. When the water-skiing season was over, we would switch to Ping-pong. We used to be fiercely competitive in that, too. Today I sometimes can beat my father in Ping-pong. And I like to rub it in a little by pointing out that he owns his own table. The one tragedy that we all shared was the death of my brother in a car accident a few years ago.

My parents were somewhat strict. I guess that I was a bad kid sometimes. But who wasn't? No one's perfect. However, I wasn't a "problem child." I haven't broken a window for years, even by accident. I never got arrested or got in trouble with the police. I was almost thirty years old before I got my first traffic ticket.

Strict or not, my parents would go into hock at Christmas time, like all other parents, and we would get wonderful presents. We also used to have the biggest Christmas tree on the block.

The thing that I remember best about my parents when I was young was their support. They were never the kind of people who went outside with me every night, playing a front-yard game of football or baseball, but they were behind what I did. They showed up at my track meets, my basketball games, and my football games.

Here I am at two years of age—probably trying to find out when the next plane will leave for the Olympic Games.

I remember one high school basketball game. It really wasn't a game—it was a scrimmage. But I was playing. It was a weekday night and nobody showed up in the stands but my mom, my dad, and a next-door neighbor.

I felt good that my parents were there. I think that parents represent the whole world to their kids, and the youngsters really appreciate it when they show up to watch a performance. That is true whether it is a basketball game, a band concert, or a debate.

My father was always a great practical joker. One of my earliest memories was something he did to me when I was about three years old. He told me a story about a monkey's head that he owned. Then he said, "Do you want to see it? I've got it down here in the closet."

We both walked down the hallway to the closet. I was so scared. Then he went into the closet and started rummaging around. He pulled out a blanket, threw the blanket over my head, and screamed, "Here it is!"

I went nuts. I was banging into walls trying to get out of that blanket. I was screaming, yelling, and crying.

Whenever I would watch a spooky movie on television, my dad would come up behind me and grab me. I would turn perfectly white and fall off the chair. My

The next year, when I was three, I posed, flashing my world-famous smile, with my aged sister Pam, who was an old lady of four.

It's only 10:25 in the morning, so all these second graders are alert. But why aren't they smiling? I'm the one with the bow tie and the suspenders.

My late brother, Burt, was two years old here. And I was all of ten. He was my pal.

dad would think that was pretty funny, and, in looking back, so do I. In some strange way, these pranks created a bond between us. And that's a bond that still exists.

I guess I got into sports in the sixth grade. I played on the basketball team. But in seventh grade, I decided to try something completely different. I went out for—are you ready for this?—the wrestling team.

I weighed 106 pounds. I also lost my first seven matches in a row. But I won the next four in a row and qualified to go to the boys' county championships. Somehow I ended up in the championship finals. In the middle of the match, both of us had bloody noses and they had to stop the match for a few minutes to stop the bleeding. P.S. I lost the match by one point.

Realizing that wrestling wasn't really my thing (I still have a tender nose), I shifted gears when I got into high school. I started out at Tarrytown High School as an outside linebacker on the football team. I also played basketball, and there is a story about that.

Basketball was never really my best sport, but I was a starter, I think, because I am left-handed. That can sometimes be an advantage in sports. I was a better player because my left hand was my good hand, and I could drive down the left side of the court. A right-hander could be in trouble doing that. The other players were as good or better than I was, but they were all right-handed. So I was always on the starting team. Of course, really good players can dribble as well with either hand. But we didn't run across that many really good players.

The fearless outside linebacker on the Tarrytown team. The only thing unusual about this shot was that my number was the same as my age.

By the way, I have one plaque that I'm pretty proud of. In 1977 I was picked as "Left-Hander of the Year" by the Left-Handers Association of America.

It was in high school that I also became a Ping-pong nut. But in my freshman year, I discovered my first love—track.

When I started, all I wanted to be was a pole-vaulter. My first try at the vault was a disaster, however. Of course I was clumsy, but I felt delighted that I soared over the bar so easily. And it was set at 8 feet 6 inches. Not bad, right?

Wrong. There I was in the air, almost 7 feet from the ground, when I remembered that I didn't know the right way to come down. I bashed my face on the bar and split my lip wide open. But when I got to our first meet, I did a little better. I cleared 8 feet without damaging myself.

By the time I was halfway through high school, my family and I were really into water-skiing, as I mentioned. I ended up winning the Eastern Water-Skiing Championship once in the junior age division and twice in the senior. My father and mother were so caught up in the sport that they bought a house in Newtown, Connecticut, because it was near the Housatonic River and great for skiing. Naturally, they also bought a boat to pull the skier.

So, in the middle of my junior year in high school, I found myself in a new home. I later played running back on the Newtown High team and filled in as quarterback. There were also the basketball and the track teams. In 1968, in my senior year, I was the Connecticut state champion in the pole vault.

Just having a little fun. But what happened to my other ski?

I thought I had it made. I waited for the offers of college scholarships to pour in. But by the end of the summer, none had. I was about ready to give up when I found out that a friend, Nick Zeoli, of Wilton, Connecticut, had talked about me to L. D. Weldon, the athletic director and track coach of Graceland College, in Lamoni, Iowa. That was the only scholarship offer I got, so I packed my bags and headed West in the fall.

Don't try to compare my athletic scholarship with what you might get at the University of Michigan or Ohio State. I was to get $500 a year. And the school tuition alone was $2,500. Besides that, I got the scholarship money only if I played in two sports.

They tried to make me a quarterback on the football team, but soon switched me to defense. In my freshman year I injured my knee in a game against Tarkio, a small college in Missouri, and never went back to the team. I did play basketball the next year, though.

But, of course, I was on the track team. Even so, it took me almost two years to find out what I really wanted to specialize in. I honestly had never thought too much about the decathlon.

The first decathlon I ever saw was the first one I ever ran in. It was at the Drake Relays, under the auspices of Drake University in Des Moines, Iowa, in the spring of 1970—in my sophomore year at Graceland. I came in sixth by scoring 6,991 points. That was encouraging, especially since it set a new record for Graceland decathletes.

I did a lot of thinking about that. I said to myself,

"If I'm ever going to do well in sports and make a mark for myself, this is my event."

The decathlon seemed as if it were made for me. In the decathlon you have to be rather good at a lot of different things. That turned me on. I have always felt that I enjoyed so many different things that I didn't want to spend all my time in just one area. Of course, other people want to be the best in the world at just one specific thing. The decathlon would turn them off. But not me.

I started to wonder whether I was physically capable of being a good decathlete. I knew that there were good decathletes who ranged in size from 5 feet 8 inches and 150 pounds to 6 feet 8 inches and 220 pounds. The larger ones would do better in the throws, but the smaller ones would do better in the runs.

However, the ideal size, if there is one, is between six feet one and six feet two, with a weight of from 190 to 205 pounds. My size, at 6 feet 2 inches and about 198 pounds, was ideal. I may be very small for a shot-putter, but I'm very large for a 1,500-meter runner. It all averages out.

I mentioned that the decathlete is not in the event for the glory. He's in it for personal satisfaction. So after those Drake Relays, I sat down and said to myself, "Boy, I know I can improve a little here and a little there. And if I can improve just a little in each event each time I compete, my score will go up and up and up."

I realized that the decathlon was the most challenging thing I had ever tried. It was just me against

My first win. I was so excited at the NAIA meet in 1971 that I don't even remember the girl walking by.

this scorecard. If I succeeded, I would get all the credit. If I failed, there would be nobody to blame but myself.

I wasn't thinking about the Olympics then. I just wanted to see how good I could get. Everyone knows that feeling. You wonder, "How good a writer can I be?" Or, "How good a musician can I be?" I wanted to know how good a decathlete I could be. I even thought that there was the chance that I might be the best in the world at something. And that something could be the decathlon.

I decided to quit all other sports and work on the decathlon all year long. I gave up football, basketball, and water-skiing, (although every once in a while I did sneak in a game of Ping-pong). I was twenty-one years old then, and the more I trained, the better I got.

My next stop was the National Association of Intercollegiate Athletics (NAIA) meet in Billings, Montana. This was in June of 1970. I scored 6,810 points and finished third. Already I was improving—in position, if not in total points.

I won my first decathlon in my junior year of college. I was at the Kansas Relays, and I scored 7,330 points. Then it was back to the Drake Relays where my score was 7,458. Unfortunately, I came in second, but I did improve my score.

I slipped a little at the next meet. It was the NAIA meet again, and I scored 7,400 points. But that time it was enough for a first-place finish.

Then came my senior year. And a big turning point. I scored 7,678 points at the Drake Relays. That was enough to qualify me to compete in the United States Olympic Trials in Eugene, Oregon, on July 3 and 4, 1972.

I never thought I had a chance to go to Munich, where the Summer Olympics were to be held, but I was certainly going to show up in Eugene.

3. My First Olympics

The reason that I got to go to the trials at all has to do with how decathletes are selected to try out. The International Olympic Committee weeds out a lot of decathletes before the trials. Every four years they set a standard of the number of points scored that would qualify you for the trials.

In 1972 the standard was 7,650 points. My 7,678 at the Drake Relays meant that I could go to Eugene.

Each country must then select its best three men for the decathlon. In the United States, that is done at the Olympic Trials. Of course, there may be some countries in which not even one person has met the qualifying standard. In that case, the country can send one person even if he has not qualified.

So one is the minimum and three is the maximum. And the United States always sends the maximum.

When I got to Eugene, I never thought that I had a chance of making the Olympic team. I didn't think that I was as good as a lot of men there. But I got lucky and had a good meet, running much better than I expected to run.

I finished third, with 7,841 points, and that made me the number three man on a three-man team. But I was on the team.

I was totally shocked. I never thought that this could happen. It seemed to me that making the Olympic team was something that always happened to the other guy. Look at me—Bruce Jenner is going to Munich!

Finally the United States Olympic team got to Munich. And finally the day of the opening ceremonies arrived. Those ceremonies are really something, and I was probably the most excited person in West Germany that day.

We all had our leisure-suit United States Olympic team parade uniforms on and we marched down to the waiting area outside the stadium. There were all the athletes from all the different countries with their uniforms on. And they were waiting to enter the stadium, too.

The United States team waited. And waited. We waited for four and one half hours. The athletes parade in, country by country, and the order is alphabetical by country. The United States is pretty far down on the list, since it begins with the letter "U." But in German, it begins with the letter "V," for *Vereinigte Staaten*, and that puts us even farther down on the list.

So there were one hundred-and-some countries ahead of us. And we stood there. And we stood there.

Finally it was our turn to march into the stadium. It was exciting, with all those other athletes there. The stadium was packed. We marched around the stadium and arrived at our place and had to stand there for about another hour while the rest of the countries came in and some more ceremonies took place.

Then came the time when the Olympic Games were declared open. After that, the last thing to happen was that thousands of pigeons were let out of their cages. Or maybe they were doves. Anyway, they were signs of peace, symbolizing the brotherhood of the Olympic Games.

Now, if you know much about pigeons, you know that when you put them in tiny cages, they are not able to relieve themselves very efficiently. So when all these birds were let out, it was awful.

Here I was, thinking about the Olympic Games and the great opening ceremonies, and these pigeons were flying over our heads. Everybody was ducking. Some of us were holding papers over our heads trying to protect ourselves from the droppings of those pigeons. But it didn't do any good.

I was a mess. I had to go back to the dormitory and send my clothes out to the cleaners.

But that is the last funny nonathletic thing that happened at the Munich Olympics. The next one was tragic.

The 1972 Munich Olympics went down in history as the "Olympics of Terror."

Someday, in a history book, the whole thing may be reduced to nothing more than a single paragraph. Something like this:

In the early hours of September 5, 1972, eight Arab guerrillas, members of the Palestinian Black September terrorist group, broke into the Israeli dormitory in Olympic Village in Munich, killing two members of the Israeli Olympic team and taking nine other members hostage. In exchange for the lives of the hostages, the terrorists demanded the release of some 200 Arab terrorists from Israeli prisons. Twenty-three hours later, after intense negotiations with West German policemen, the terrorists and their hostages were conveyed to the Munich airport. There, just before midnight, a shootout erupted. After it was over, five terrorists, a policeman, and all nine hostages were dead—the latter apparently killed by the terrorists. The Games were suspended during the day of September 5 and on September 6 for a memorial service for the slain athletes held in the stadium. A few hours later, after considerable controversy, the Games were resumed, coming to an end on September 11 in a somewhat subdued atmosphere.

I first heard about what was going on while I was brushing my teeth in the dormitory on that awful Tuesday morning. Steve Prefontaine, the great American track star (who was later killed in an automobile accident), rushed into the lavatory. He told me that someone had been killed in another part of the Olympic Village.

We soon found out that it had happened in the Israeli dormitory. I had met some Puerto Rican athletes in the Village, and I knew that their dormitory was right across from the Israeli dormitory. So I went over there. From the Puerto Rican dorm, we could see, from time to time, the head of a terrorist—one of the men who were holding the Israelis hostage.

Hours later, after the massacre was over, I was angry. And, to tell you the truth, I was angry for a very selfish reason. I was thinking, "Who are these guys coming in here and ruining *my* Olympic Games? I have trained for years to be here and now we have some people who have never even run half a mile in their lives blowing people away and disrupting the whole games."

You see, I was very concerned about running the decathlon on September 7 and 8. As the whole international incident progressed, I got angry for another reason.

Avery Brundage, an American and the head of the International Olympic Committee at the time, had made a decision. Although there were many people all over the world who thought that the Games should have been canceled out of respect for the Israeli dead, he disagreed. He ordered that after a brief period of mourning the Games should go on. For this decision, he was criticized all over the world.

I said that I got angry for a different reason. I became angry at the people who disagreed with Brundage. This was not, at the time, a popular view. And even today it is not a popular view. But I look at it this way.

I felt that the best thing that could happen would be for the athletes to resume the games and perform as well as possible. That would show the world that a group of insane murderers could not disrupt the events. If the games had been canceled, it would mean that we all had played right into the hands of the criminals.

What they wanted was for the games to be canceled. That would have riveted the world's attention on their cause and proved that they were more powerful than they really were. Everyone would have remembered the 1972 Olympics as the ones that were stopped by a handful of terrorists. And think about this: What would they have done for an encore?

Eight years later, I still feel the same. I don't think that the Olympic Games should be used for political reasons. There are, unfortunately, politics involved with the Games because politicians run them. If the athletes could run them, there would be fewer problems.

You see, the Olympic athletes get along so well together. Nikolai Avilov may be from the Soviet Union and Guido Kratschmer may be from West Germany, but I think of them only as top-notch decathletes. They are in the same boat that I am. They like to win as much as I do. They may have the names of different countries across their chests, but they are like me in most ways.

The person watching the Games on television may hear the announcer saying, "The Russian is in the lead, but the West German is coming up on him." We don't think of it like that. Avilov of the Soviet Union may be out in the lead, but that's Nikolai, not "the Russian."

I don't think, "I'm an American. I have to beat that Russian." I think, "I'm an athlete. I'm going to beat that other athlete."

Off the field we athletes are friends. We have good times together even when we can't speak the other people's languages. Also, you may end up competing with them for years. You may even go all over the world and run into them at every meet.

There is, of course, the possibility that decathletes know each other better than any other type of Olympic athlete. We do spend a lot of time with each other. For example, if there are as few as a dozen of us entered and we are going through the long jump, we may have to wait twenty minutes between tries. And we may spend that time talking to each other.

What happens in that situation is that you get warmed up, you jump, and then you have to get all warmed up again, twenty minutes later, for your next try. By the way, that also gives you time to psych yourself out of a good jump. In any case, we all spend a lot of time together. That's why we know each other so well. That's why I think that the Olympics would be better off being run by the athletes.

The Olympic Games are the biggest athletic meet this world has. Only the Olympics are watched by people the world over. Only a few countries are interested in our World Series. Very few people in the United States are interested in the World Cup soccer matches. But most every nation is interested in the Olympics—all over the globe.

So politicians, with the world looking on, use the Games to better the cause of their countries or, at least, to get headlines. That may be why there are so many political problems connected with the Olympics.

Back to me at Munich. I didn't win even a bronze medal. But I didn't expect to win. I did, however, make myself a promise. If I didn't come in in the top ten, I would give up the decathlon. Guess what. I came in tenth.

I accumulated 7,722 points, almost as many as I had scored in the Olympic Trials. Avilov was way up there ahead of me, in first place, with his 8,454.

The main thing was that I had learned a lot. That pleased me. Remember that I had been running the decathlon for only about two years. Now I had learned what the Olympic Games were all about. I had been preparing myself by standing around in the background watching what was going on.

When the Olympics started, I was scared. Then I learned that fear is not all that bad. It gets you psyched up for what you have to do. You learn to deal with pressure that way.

Anyway, I made myself another promise. Since I had come in in the top ten, I said to myself, "You're going to Montreal four years from now."

4. In the Meantime

Most people probably think that being in the Munich Olympics in 1972 was the most important thing that happened to me that year. They're wrong. The big event that year was my marriage to Chrystie Anne Crownover on December 16.

If it hadn't been for Chrystie, my life would have been vastly different. Remember that I had decided that I was going back to the Olympics. I said that I would give up anything in order to prepare myself. Without her I would not have been able to do it.

She and I both knew that, win, lose, or draw, I was quitting the decathlon right after the Montreal Games were over in 1976. And, of course, I would quit sooner if I didn't make the team.

She was behind me all the way. Actually, she was behind me even before we were married. I hadn't been what you might call an outstanding scholar at Graceland. But she was. And after I started dating her and she began helping me with my homework, my grades went up. I made the dean's list both semesters of my senior year. To this day we have a family joke. She

asks me, "If we ever split up, which one of us gets custody of your college diploma?"

After we were married, I went so deep into training that Chrystie had to do almost everything else. She took over the checkbook. She ran the house. She cooked the meals. She kept me away from reporters when necessary. She turned down personal appearance requests when I couldn't bring myself to disappoint someone. She was tough.

Also, she brought home most of the money.

Chrystie became a flight attendant for United Airlines to support the family. And that caused a problem for us. We had figured that we would be living in Connecticut near my folks. So she got assigned to the New York City operations at United. But I had to stay in Lamoni for the rest of the school year to do my student teaching, so that I could get a teaching license. So she spent that whole semester commuting from New York to Iowa.

There was one great thing about her being a flight attendant, though. They do get airline passes. So Chrystie could get to most of the places where I was competing. Having her there was very important to me. And, I think, important to our marriage.

In the spring of 1973, we decided not to move to Connecticut. We moved to San Jose, California. The

Here is the wedding picture. I've always thought that Chrystie looked like a princess, while I was obviously trying out for the monster part in Frankenstein. *By the way, take a look at that bridal dress. Chrystie made it herself.*

The moment of triumph—graduation day.

Honestly, flight attendants don't fly the planes—except in disaster movies. Chrystie was just clowning around.

weather there was better for training, and San Jose probably has more track people in training per square mile than any other town in the world. And track people like to hang around together to exchange training tips.

Chrystie and I had no place to live, and even if we had, we would have had no furniture to go into the place. But we did finally get settled in and even bought a car. It was a Porsche 914 sports car, the least expensive model that Porsche made. But I loved that car. I even promised myself that, if I won the Olympics, I would get the best Porsche, a Turbo Carrera. Gold colored, of course, to go with my medal.

I worked a bit in San Jose. We could use a little more money than Chrystie could bring in. I had worked with my father when I was in high school and during summer vacations while I was in college, so I got a job with a San Jose tree surgeon.

That wasn't exactly what I thought I wanted to do with my life, so I went into selling real estate and life insurance. Later, I gave up the real estate and stuck to life insurance. It seemed to be a good business to be in after the Olympics were over.

I found that I could sell my quarterly quota in a week or so, and then take the next ten or eleven weeks off for training. I would only have to work when a customer had a problem. New England Life Insurance never complained about this arrangement. They were very good to me.

Working part time didn't bother me. The Olympics were the important thing. I figured that after the Olympics I would have forty or fifty more years to make something of myself in business.

Things were not all peaches and cream at first. The 1973 track season was a disaster for me. First I had back trouble and then I broke some bones in my foot.

Then came the 1974 season. Things started going right. I started out the season by winning the Kansas Relays decathlon with 8,240 points. This was the first time I had beaten that old 8,000-point barrier. In May I scored 7,998 points in the Santa Barbara Invitational Championship. That was below 8,000, but I won.

The next month, I set a personal record of 8,245 points in the Amateur Athletics Union (AAU) meet. That was not only a winning score but also a new AAU record. In August, in a team decathlon competition against decathletes from the Soviet Union and West Germany held in Estonia, I finished first with 8,308 points, and the American team won.

At the end of the 1974 season I had been undefeated. And I was ranked number one in the world. What a year.

In 1975 I started out by scoring 8,138 points to take first in the decathlon in the Drake Relays. I followed that up with a first place score of 8,045 points in Paris. What do you know? Bruce Jenner was now the French National Champion. And I don't even speak the language.

I was feeling pretty cocky. Then I suffered my comedown at the AAU championships in July in Santa

Ever loyal to San Jose. Note the printing on my track shirt. Chrystie and me with Telly Savalas.

Barbara, California. I had won all my meets in the previous year and a half. But on that awful July day, I didn't feel the old fire burning deep down inside.

I just couldn't start the fire. I was excited about the meet, but I just wasn't operating at 100 per cent. I also knew that I hadn't been scoring as well in 1975 as I had in 1974.

It was time for the pole vault—my specialty. Fifteen minutes before, I was jumping perfectly in practice. But when it came time for the event, I raced three times down the runway toward the line and I couldn't get off the ground. To this day, I don't know why that happened. I never even got anywhere near the bar.

Usually I am in control of myself. But this time I lost my cool completely. I had scored zero points in the pole vault and had no chance of having a decent decathlon score, much less of winning the title.

I threw my pole and accidentally almost took a cameraman's head off. I said a few words I probably shouldn't have. I stomped out of the pit. I ran across the infield and across the track on the other side of the field. I headed right out of the stadium.

I found a big clump of trees out there and I cried my eyes out. I was thinking, "What has happened?" I had completely lost control of myself. I was underneath those trees for a long time, not only crying but also cursing myself.

Then I tried to evaluate my performance. I wasn't just thinking about the pole vault. I asked myself, "Why have you fouled up when you are in better shape than you have ever been? Why are you scoring fewer points than you did last year? Why can't you get excited about decathlon meets?"

Here I was working out six to eight hours every day trying to improve and yet my performance was going downhill. I thought that maybe I shouldn't have put all my eggs in one basket—training for the Olympics. I thought that maybe I should keep the insurance business going since I obviously was going nowhere in sports.

Then Chrystie found me under those trees. I cried some more and pretty much told her how I felt. It was good to get that off my chest. Somehow I got myself under control and we went back into the stadium.

But I didn't perform in any other event that day. I didn't even want to see a decathlon at that point. And this was just thirteen months before the Olympic Games. It was not the best timing in the world.

For the next few nights, Chrystie and I talked about what was going on. Finally, it was Chrystie who came up with an answer. But she put it in the form of a couple of questions.

First she asked, "Do you want to win in the Olympic Games?"

I said, chuckling a bit, "Of course I want to win in the Olympic Games. I'm spending six to eight hours a day working out. Of course I want to win. I'm still rated number one in the world."

Chrystie said, "Okay. I accept that. Now, one more question. Is winning in the Olympic Games the most important thing in your life?"

That was a mind-blowing question. It would have been easy for me to say, "Yes, it is." But Chrystie and I have always been honest with each other. I couldn't honestly say yes at that moment. I had to think it over. I had to sit down and search my mind for a while.

I sat back in the chair and remembered how I had thought just a few days before about keeping the insur-

Chrystie and I finally got my problem straightened out. I'm in the middle here. That's Bertha at the bottom of the picture.

ance business going so that, if I didn't win, I would have something to fall back on. I began to think that, at that moment, winning was really not the most important thing in my life. Maybe the insurance business was. Or at least it seemed to be important enough to take away some of the importance of winning in the Olympics.

But I knew I wanted the Olympics. I had even set a goal for myself. I wanted to score 8,500 points. That would break the world record. And I wanted to do it before the Olympic Games. Still, I couldn't honestly say that winning in the Olympics was the most important thing in my life.

I thought to myself, "What if I do decide that winning in the Olympics *is* the most important thing in my life? I would be risking a tremendous amount. I would be risking my pride in myself. I would be risking years of my life."

That was a heavy thing to decide. Then I thought, "What happens if I lose?"

If I decided that winning was so important, losing would hurt all the more. I would not have been competing just for the fun of it. I would have been competing for the gold medal and then lose it.

Then I thought, "If I lose, I'll deal with losing, starting on the day that the decathlon ends. It may take me a day to recover. It may take me twenty years of

The flight attendant and the hopeful athlete on a visit back home in Connecticut. (Photo from the Newtown *Bee*)

Chrystie running out to meet me. She doesn't seem to know whether to laugh or to cry.

I felt pretty confident at the Tri-Country Track Meet in Eugene, Oregon, where athletes from the United States, the Soviet Union, and Poland competed.

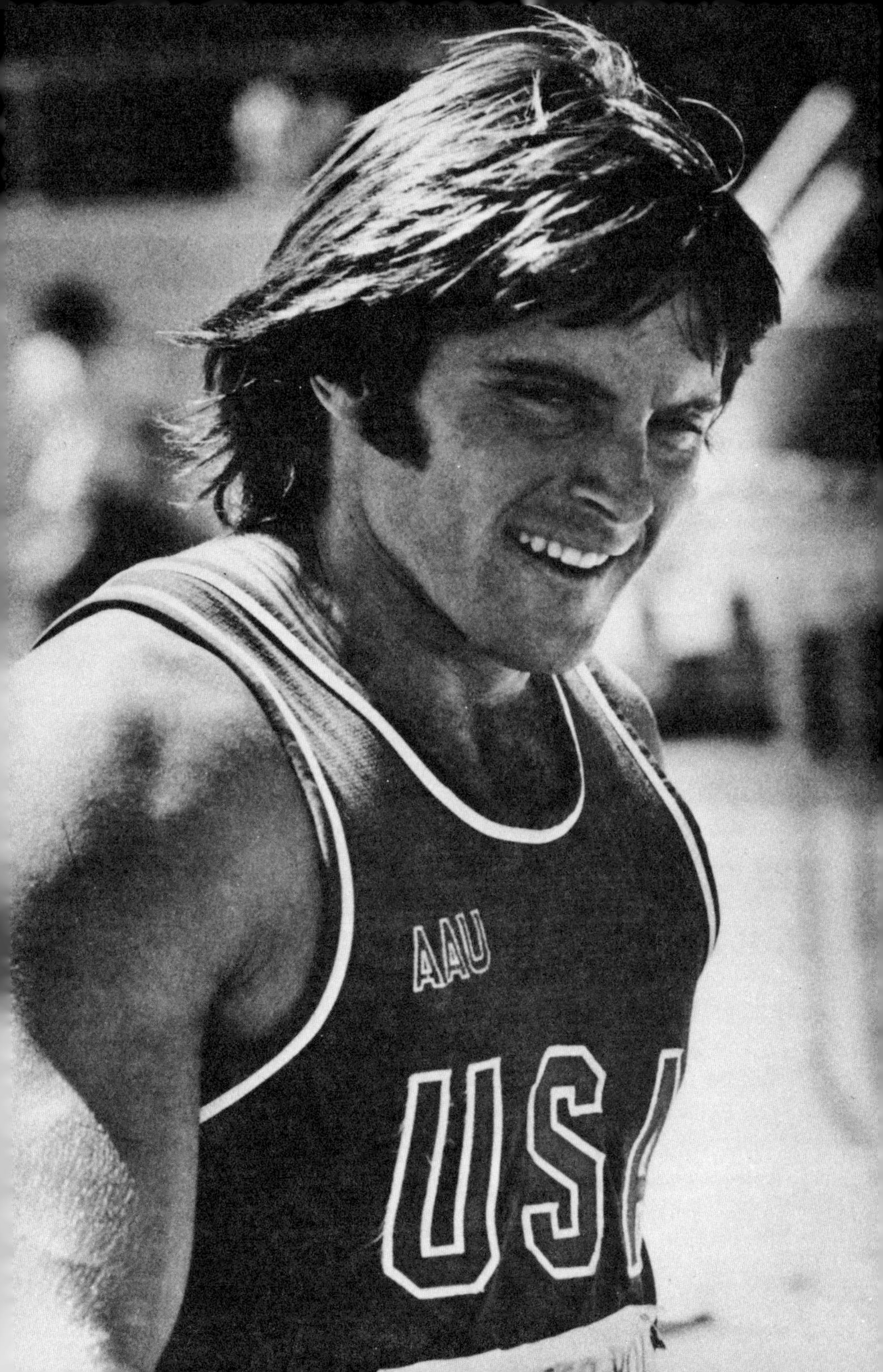
AAU

The end of my turning-point meet at Eugene. The officials, as you can see, were a little bit less formal than Olympic officials tend to be. They let Chrystie up there with me. Fred Dixon of the United States finished second, and the man on my right, who finished third, is Nikolai Avilov. I never was too good at opening champagne. (Pearl Street Photo-Graphics, Hudson-Renken Associates, Inc.)

my life to recover. But I have enough confidence in myself as a person to know that, some day or other, I will recover."

So, if it happened, I knew that I could do something else with my life. I knew that losing was not the same as dying, and I could go back to the insurance business or go into sports broadcasting or something else. I was convinced that I would be able to pick up the pieces.

Now I could tell Chrystie, "Yes, winning in the Olympics *is* the most important thing in my life."

Wow! As soon as I said that, something happened. I was just sitting in the chair, and suddenly the adrenaline started pumping through me. I got so excited, just sitting there. It was as if someone had turned on a hose that hadn't been turned on all year. I had finally made a commitment to myself.

And Chrystie and I made a pact. Whenever I won a meet, she would be sure to be the first one to run out and greet me.

My next meet was at Eugene, Oregon, one month later, in August. I got down on that track and I was going for everything. I was hungry. I was 100 per cent again. My stomach was twisting and turning. I almost felt like throwing up.

At a time like that, all you want to do is run and get to the finish line. The result? I won the decathlon and broke the world record by scoring 8,524 points. I beat the other decathletes in every event by 300 or 400 points.

GO
JENNER
GO

After the meet, it took me a month or six weeks to come down off the high that I had felt. I didn't even sleep for a couple of nights after the meet.

But losing sleep is not all that important to me. I'm not a big sleeper. Sometimes I get as little as two or three hours a night. I just lie there and relax.

After the first day of a decathlon, when the first five events are over, I may get no sleep at all. I used to worry about that. I used to lie there thinking, "Here I am, trying to win tomorrow, and I should be sleeping."

I don't worry anymore about not sleeping. I just lie there all night, thinking of my strategy for the next day. I never would want to take a chance on sleeping pills.

In October of 1975, I was on the United States team at the Pan-American Games in Mexico City. I came in first with 8,015 points. And I was still ranked number one in the world.

Then, in 1976, it was back to the Drake Relays. The result was first place with 8,230 points.

Next stop. My last meet in the United States. It was the Olympic Trials in Eugene, Oregon. What a meet. I finished first and broke my own world record with 8,538 points. I was so delighted that I took two days off from training.

Chrystie with her GO JENNER GO T-shirt. I'm getting ready for a running event. Notice how popular the decathlon was. What happened to all the spectators?

One of the things that spurred me on in that meet was the family. Chrystie, my folks, and her folks all were wearing yellow T-shirts that said GO JENNER GO on the back.

So now it was official. Chrystie and I were going to be spending part of the summer in Montreal.

5. My Second Olympics

Chrystie and I made our plans. Of course, she was going with me. And so was Bertha, our Labrador. We felt that, since Bertha had been my coach all through training, running with me every day, the least we could do was to take her with us.

About a month before the Olympic Games, I was scheduled to go to Plattsburg, New York, about twenty-five miles south of the Canadian border, to train with the United States track and field team. Before I left, I washed and waxed my Porsche. Then I covered it with a heavy cloth wrapper. I wanted it to be fresh and clean for us when we came back the next month.

Strangely enough, I had to go to Montreal before I went to Plattsburg, knowing full well that I would be going back to Montreal very soon. You see, Montreal is the closest city to Plattsburg that has an airport with flights in from California.

We landed at Montreal and then hopped a bus to Plattsburg. That was a trip of ninety miles. And, compared with the ride back to Montreal a few weeks later, it was peaceful.

The American decathlete with his coach, Bertha. (Photo by Dave Drennan)

So I left Chrystie and Bertha and trained with the team for those weeks. Finally it was time to pack up and head for Canada. That was a trip I will never forget.

Because of what had happened at Munich four years before, the Canadians had set up the strictest security ever for the Montreal Olympics. We got on the buses, and from Plattsburg to the Canadian border we had a New York State police escort. But that was nothing compared to what we encountered when we crossed into Canada.

We were met by Canadian police cars and motorcycle escorts. Helicopters were hovering overhead. So here we were in this heavily armed caravan. Every intersection had been blocked off. No other vehicles were on the freeway with us. It was unbelievable.

Even in the Olympic Village where we stayed, things were a little disconcerting at first. Everywhere uniformed men were walking around with guns. After a while, though, all of us got used to being guarded twenty-four hours a day.

However, I must admit that I had a little nagging fear. I thought about it a lot, and I guess Chrystie thought about it even more than I did.

You are out in the open when you are down there on the field. And someone could take a potshot at you without much trouble. I could get to the finish line in the 1,500-meter run and somebody in the stands with a gun could do me in. There was little or no security up there in the stands.

I'm always interested in food, but Chrystie seems to have had it all. (Photo by Anne Kerschner)

Of course, looking on the bright side, it would be a little bit more difficult hitting me when I was pole-vaulting. The assassin would have to aim for me on the rise. And, unless he had been an expert trapshooter, he would have missed.

Our living conditions were excellent. Twelve athletes were put into two-bedroom, one-bathroom apartments. That may sound crowded, but we didn't spend too much time in our apartments.

Also, you get fed well at the Olympics. Some of the heavy fellows—the weight-lifters and the shot-putters—might eat three or four steaks and a quart of mashed potatoes for lunch. But I stuck to carbohydrates.

Then came the time of practicing and the time of psyching myself up. I consider the decathlon to be 80 per cent a mental challenge and only 20 per cent a physical challenge. That is, of course, if I am in tip-top shape. And at Montreal I was physically ready. I had been working on the physical aspects of the decathlon for years. Now it was time to put in the final work on the mental aspect.

Mentally, I knew every step I was going to take once I got inside the Olympic Stadium for the decathlon. The only things that might stop me from performing well were pressure or some unexpected circumstances that might happen during the Games and throw me off mentally.

You have to take the decathlon one event at a time. And you have to prepare mentally for ten different events that require different types of mental preparation. In one way, it's like being a golfer. If a golfer does well on the first hole, he or she has another one coming up immediately. And the golfer has to forget that first hole.

It's even a little bit worse for the decathlete. He starts off as a sprinter, then he must turn himself into a long-jumper, then a shot-putter, etc. Each event is a complete change from what you have just done. You go from runner to jumper to thrower. So, mentally, you have to make a complete change in your attitude between each event.

Things can happen during a meet. Maybe in the first two or three events you do tremendously well. You can get so high that you stop thinking. You just let the adrenaline flow. And that can work against you. The adrenaline is pumping, but the next thing that you know, you have made three bad throws in the shot.

Or you may start out and not do too well in the first two or three events. The worst thing that can happen to you is to run a bad 100-meter, the first event. You think, "Well, I'm slow today." Then there is the long jump staring you in the face. You have to get up a good head of steam in that event, and if you think you are slow, it will affect your performance.

So you have to forget your past performance between each event. This takes concentration and a good mental attitude. The only way you can improve your concentration and your attitude is through practice. And I had had that practice. I was ready.

Then came the morning of July 29, 1976. I wasn't able to eat much for breakfast, since this was the day when the decathlon would start.

I went back to my apartment and started gathering my equipment together. It was almost like packing for a three-week trip to Europe. I needed my towels, a jug of Gatorade, two pairs of socks, some elastic bandages and body wrapping, and my shoes.

I wore Adidas at the Olympics, probably because the Bruce Jenner line of shoes had not been started yet. And there were a lot of them. For the first day, I packed five pairs. First of all there was a pair of warm-up shoes. These are flat-soled, and I wear them only between events to walk around in. Then there was a pair of sprinting shoes. They are lightweight, with spikes, and are used in the 100-meter and 400-meter runs. I would also use them for the 110-meter hurdles on the next day.

The third pair was my long-jump shoes. These have bottoms that are slightly raised toward the heel and give you a forward rocking movement on takeoff. Then there was a pair with flexible rubber bottoms that I would use in the shot put today and the discus tomorrow. Finally, there was a pair in which the sole of the right shoe was higher than the left. This gives one better leverage in the high jump.

I left behind my other three pairs, since I wouldn't need them until the next day. One of them was my pole-vaulting pair. They are heavier than most track shoes so that they will not rip under the strain of the takeoff. Then there was a pair of javelin boots, high-laced to give me ankle support. Finally there was a pair that seem to be my security blanket. They were three years old and all beat up and were to be used in the 1,500-meter run.

I went for a rubdown and then started to warm up at the practice track. I felt good. I was running smoothly and strongly. I knew I would perform well.

Now it was time to go to the stadium. The first thing that happened was that I was inspected by a crew from the International Olympic Committee. They checked my shoes, measuring the length of the spikes and the height of the soles. They checked my number—good old 935—on my uniform shirt and shorts. Finally, they put a strip of adhesive tape over the ADIDAS stamped on my shoes. Olympic athletes are amateurs; that means no advertising.

Then came the 100-meter run. I ran it in 10.94 seconds. This was not as good as my own personal record—I had once run the event in 10.7—but Avilov of the Soviet Union, the decathlon champion in 1972 and the man I thought I had to beat in 1976, had a disastrous time—11.23 seconds.

I felt confident. Before each new event in the decathlon, since I had decided to retire after the Olympics, I would say to myself, "This is the last time you are going to do this. So do it right." And I could feel the adrenaline flowing.

I felt even more confident after the long jump. My distance was 23 feet 8¼ inches, only 4 inches shorter than my own personal record. That put me in sixth place and 10 points ahead of Avilov. Guido Kratschmer of West Germany was in first place. And I was only 105 points behind him.

I must admit that I was worried about the shot put. I had hurt my hand and I didn't know how I would do. Guess what happened. I set a new personal record. I put the shot 50 feet 4¼ inches—the best I had ever done. That shoved me way up in the standings. I was now in second place, only 69 points behind Kratschmer.

By this time I began thinking that my father would be getting worried. We had made a deal. If I won, he had to quit smoking.

I set another personal record in the high jump. My jump was 6 feet 8 inches. Even so, I slipped in the standings to third place. Avilov had cleared 7 feet ¼ inch and had moved into second. But I was only 51 points behind him and still only 69 points behind Kratschmer.

At the end of the day came the 400-meter run. I came in first, setting yet another personal record—47.5 seconds; Kratschmer and Avilov were each more than a ½ second behind me. I was still in third place, but only 17 points behind Avilov and 35 behind Kratschmer. Things were beginning to get exciting.

The next day started out as a minidisaster in the 110-meter hurdles. My time was 14.84 seconds. That was not bad for me, but Avilov did it in 14.2 and Kratschmer in 14.56. I was still in third place, but

Avilov had taken over first and was 90 points ahead. Kratschmer, falling into second place, had widened the gap on me, too. He was now 64 points ahead.

I got back into second place after the discus throw. My distance was 164 feet 1 inch. Now I was only 9 points behind Avilov and 18 points ahead of Kratschmer.

Then came my specialty, the pole vault. I vaulted 15 feet 9 inches—and I went in front to stay. Kratschmer took over second place, 66 points behind. Avilov was 76 points behind me.

I threw the javelin 224 feet 10 inches. That put me 188 points ahead of Kratschmer and 249 ahead of Avilov.

The 1,500-meter run was the last event. I didn't win it, but I ran second, only about 4 yards behind the leader. Actually, my 4 minutes 12.3 seconds was another personal record.

I had won the whole decathlon with 8,618 points, a new world record. Kratschmer came in second and Avilov was third.

After twelve years of training, I had actually *won* the thing. When I crossed the finish line of the 1,500-meter run, the last event, my hands went up in the air, and I screamed as loud as I could. I felt this giant release. It was over with. If you have seen my

My moment of exultation—crossing the finish line of the 1,500-meter run. The gold medal was mine. (Sports Illustrated Photo by Walter Iooss, Jr.)

USA
935

picture crossing the finish line, you have seen my expression. I look as if I had stuck my finger into a light socket. I had won.

The best part of it was that I knew that they could never take that away from me. It was mine. The gold medal was mine. The Olympic Championship was mine. All those feelings, all those memories were mine. And no matter what happened to me for the rest of my life, I had done it.

People asked me why I waved that little American flag after I had won the decathlon. First of all, it wasn't mine—some guy ran out on the track and handed it to me. After I took it, I said to myself, "Oh, no. What do I do now?"

If I had thrown it away, it would have been an international incident. So I waved it.

Ordinarily, I'm not a flag-waver. Of course, I've been all over the world and I still feel that there is no place like home. I would never want to live any place else but the United States. But when people ask, "Did you win that gold medal for you or for your country?" I have to say that it was for me.

I was the one out there doing all the work, training all the time. But I think that what my country did for me was to give me the opportunity to grow up to do what I wanted to do. I was honored to wear "USA" across my chest.

The tough part of winning came maybe fifteen or twenty minutes after the 1,500-meter race was over. They walked us decathletes out from underneath the

Olympic Stadium, across the track, into the center of the stadium. And there was the victory platform right in front of us. It was a big white thing. And there were two steps up to the top of the platform.

I looked at those steps and I thought to myself, "Those are the last steps of your career."

I was retiring after the Olympics were over. So I started crying. I thought of all those years that I had been working, of the training that had consumed my whole life for so long.

And when I made those last two steps to get to the top of the platform, it would all be over with. It would all be done.

Finally, they announced that I was the Olympic decathlon champion. I walked up those two steps. I got to the top. I felt good. I was really satisfied. I had accomplished everything in the decathlon that I could ever do. There was nothing else left. There was nothing bigger than winning in the Olympic Games and breaking a world record.

I knew at that point that I could walk away. I was ready to leave it to the next man to win the next Olympic decathlon.

Then I heard our national anthem. That was the final part of my dream come true. I had always imagined that I would hear "The Star-Spangled Banner" being played for me in the Olympic Stadium. That was the ending to my happy story.

I was in seventh heaven. The official had to say to me, "You're going to have to get down." So I got down. And I walked across back from the center of the stadium. And it was over with.

(By the way, when I won, my dad did give up smoking. That lasted about three weeks.)

When I walked off the field after the medal ceremony, I glanced around one more time and then walked away. That was the end of the decathlon for me. I never even went back to get my vaulting poles. I left them in the stadium. They're a hassle to travel with and I was finished with them.

6. And After

How did my family react? Chrystie was as delirious as I was. And my parents were extremely excited about the whole thing. They naturally felt more tension before the Games than after. When the thing was over, they were proud, but they treated me just as they always had.

Chrystie's folks reacted differently. They had been living in San Jose when we did, and the four of us were great friends. We didn't see them very often, but we did visit each other regularly. I also used to play golf occasionally with Chrystie's dad, Carlos.

About two weeks after the games were over, Chrystie's mother came to see her in San Jose and began crying her eyes out. The first thing she said to Chrystie was "I wonder if Bruce will ever play golf with Carlos again."

Here I was, being thought of by my in-laws as a big star—someone who had appeared on television. And we all know that people who appear on TV are not real . . . You can be sure that Carlos and I went out and played golf that weekend.

My mother and father do look a little proud of me, don't they? (Photo by Anne Kerschner)

But to say that winning the Olympic decathlon changed my life is an understatement. About two months after the games, I thought back and counted up the unreal things I had done since Montreal.

I had been the guest on four different national TV talk shows and variety shows. I had played tennis on national TV, teaming up with Rafer Johnson, the 1960 Olympic decathlon champion. We had played Ethel Kennedy and Jean Kennedy Smith; we lost.

I had spent four days with my father in a Louisiana swamp. We were working with an alligator relocation crew and being photographed by a film crew from the television show, "The American Sportsman."

I had had dinner at the White House. President Gerald Ford's wife Betty, sat right beside me.

I had gone back to Newtown, Connecticut, where they renamed the football field "Bruce Jenner Stadium." I had signed six hundred autographs (a new personal record) at the opening of a Philadelphia shopping center.

I had signed a two-year contract with the American Broadcasting Company to be both a sports commentator and an actor.

Finally, I had been flown to Italy to do a screen test in Rome for the title role in the movie *Superman*. I flunked out because I photograph too young. They wanted someone who looked as if he were in his late thirties. But it was fun wearing the cape for a while.

My first job for ABC was as a commentator on the "Battle of the Network Stars" program. On one of those shows, Howard Cosell really did a job on me.

To Bruce Jenner
With best wishes, Gerald R. Ford

Being invited to the White House was a thrill. You can probably guess who the other guy in a tuxedo is, and if you look between us, you will see the right eye of Shirley Temple Black. Meeting her was a pleasure, too.

What did I say on TV? Chrystie seems puzzled, and I don't know whether Mike Douglas is laughing or sneezing. (Photo by Arthur Manfredi)

We televised "Battle of the Network Stars" at Pepperdine University, in Malibu, just a few blocks from my house. That meant I didn't have to get up so early in the morning. That's Howard Cosell, the ABC sportscaster, with me in the middle of the back row. How many other television personalities can you name?

They had one of those sideshow stunts—the one where a clown sits on a bar over a big tank of water. Then someone throws a ball at a little target. If the ball hits the target, the bar collapses and the clown goes into the water. You've all seen the trick.

They put me on the bar over the water and Howard was supposed to give a statement about what was coming up on the show. Then he was to throw the ball at my target. They had a wire hooked up to the bar from behind so that when Howard threw the ball, they would pull the wire and I would fall in the water whether he hit the target or not.

Now, I thought that Howard couldn't hit the broad side of a barn. But even so, I knew I was going swimming.

Howard took a couple of practice throws. They were terrible. Not even close. Then he turned to Bob Conrad, the television actor that he was interviewing, and said, "When the tape is rolling, I'll hit the target." That broke up Conrad, and even I joined in the laughter.

Sure enough, when the cameras were rolling, Howard turned around, wound up, and threw the ball. He nailed the target right in the center. I went into the water and Howard got a standing ovation.

Everyone who saw that show probably thinks that it took twenty or thirty takes before we got that shot. To this day, Howard never lets me forget that story.

Howard Cosell is a great guy. He was the man who helped me the most when I was learning my trade

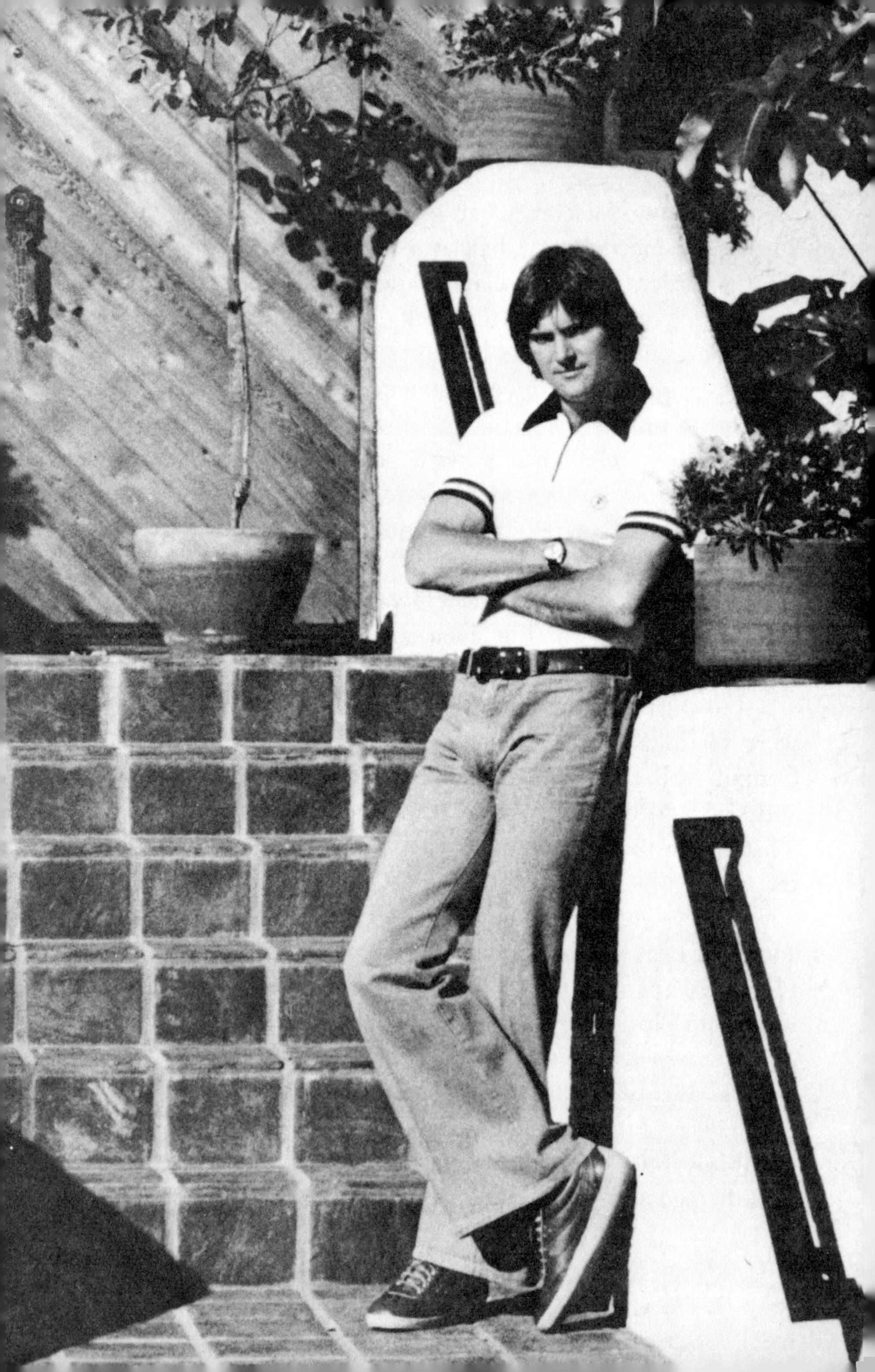

of sportscaster. He was always helping me improve my stage presence and telling me how I was coming across. Two other sportscasting superstars also were my very kind teachers. I'm referring to Keith Jackson and Frank Gifford.

After the Olympics, we moved from San Jose to Malibu and bought our first house. Besides Chrystie and me, there are three other members of the family who live in the house. First of all, there is our son, little Burt, named for my late brother. He was born in September of 1978. Then there are the dogs. Bertha is still around, and so is her son, Barney. They are both great Frisbee players.

We love it in Malibu. When I was a very little kid I didn't know about California weather. I lived in the East and I didn't really know that somewhere it doesn't snow in the winter. I also didn't know that the people on the West Coast had a different life-style from ours in the East. I could say that I didn't know what was going on in the rest of the world.

Now I have traveled all over much of the Western world and yet I like it best in California. We prefer Malibu because it is more private and has an athletic life-style. And that's what we want. We want a bit of property with some privacy because we live a very public life. That makes us value our private life even more.

Here I am in front of our first house in Malibu.

The proud parents with little Burt. He doesn't seem to be too interested.

We are not the Beverly Hills types who can't even go to the grocery store without getting dressed up. Here in Malibu you can go to the store barefoot and wearing jeans. It's more of a beachy type atmosphere than a Los Angeles type of atmosphere.

But it's close enough to Los Angeles for us to be able to get to everything in minutes. I can work and do what I have to do right here.

When you are in the television business, you have to live in either the Los Angeles or the New York area. And I could not live in New York. I even have trouble spending a day there. As soon as I have finished my business in New York, I'm in the first cab to the airport and on my way home.

I guess it's because I like dirt. And I don't like cement. I like trees and openness. If you work in New York, the only way to get this openness is to go all the way to Westchester County or Connecticut. Those areas are nice, and I lived there myself as a child. But now I can really enjoy myself.

We can even have snow in winter if we want it. We can go to nearby ski areas or up to Lake Tahoe. And if we don't want the snow, we don't have to have it. We can stay right in Malibu.

One big advantage in being retired from sports is that you can relax and have more fun. When you are an athlete, your body is the most important thing to you. Most people, for example, who wake up in the morning with a sore toe can forget about it. But the athlete has to worry.

I finally made it to Yale—as a guest speaker, not as a student. (Photo by Anne Kerschner)

He or she needs that toe in perfect shape. The athlete has to watch out for drafts lest he or she get a cold. The athlete has to give up eating some kinds of food because there is that old athletic diet.

But now I'm retired and I can pretty much eat what I want. I get three decent meals a day. No one tells me not to eat that pasta or that hamburger. But I'm still eating my Wheaties, as I've done since I was a kid.

Both Chrystie and I really do *eat them.* (Photo by Wagner International Photos, Inc.)

I can eat all kinds of things. Take a Big Mac. One of those every once in a while is not bad. It has meat, bread, lettuce, and so on. It is certainly better for you than many types of food that people stuff into their mouths.

I like all kinds of pasta; my favorites are spaghetti and lasagna. My favorite drink is milk.

To tell the truth, I didn't take my diet too

seriously even when I was in training. I never checked my calories or my protein intakes. I did try to eat three good meals a day because I was a lot more active and so a lot hungrier than I am now.

Now, if I'm working, I may not have lunch. I can even survive on only one meal a day. Sometimes I think that eating can be a waste of time.

Here is an example of my diet. It was a fairly typical day for me. I got up and had a bowl of Wheaties. I put bananas and milk on the cereal and just a little sugar on top. Then I didn't have any lunch at all.

In the evening I had a bowl of Chrystie's delicious broccoli soup and a couple of meat balls left over from the previous day's spaghetti dinner. This was washed down with a couple of glasses of milk.

Just before bed I had a bowl of ice cream.

Usually, I just eat what is around the house. If there is fruit, I'll eat fruit. If there are cookies, I'll eat cookies—chocolate chip, of course.

So you can see I really don't worry about my diet as long as I feel well. But it seems that I often have better things to do with my time than eat. I would rather be doing something active than eating. Chrystie likes to eat, but she is as casual about it as I am.

The funny thing is, even though I am no longer in training, I keep losing weight, not gaining it. I'm now about ten pounds lighter than I was at the Olympics.

One of the greatest things dawned on me right after I retired. It happened the first time I played tennis after the Olympics. I got a little cramp in a leg muscle and immediately thought that I had to sit down and rest until the cramp went away.

Then I realized that I had retired and didn't have to worry about that cramp. I could go on playing if I wanted and maybe walk around with a sore leg for a while. My legs were no longer my career. I just needed them to walk around on. So I kept playing tennis that day. What a feeling of freedom I had.

To sum up my attitude about physical fitness, today staying in shape comes second. The decathlon is behind me. My business activities come first.

I do lift weights, and I play tennis all the time. Actually, I lead a very active life, but I'm just not on a schedule anymore.

If I find the time for exercise, I exercise. Unless I can find a tennis court when I'm on the road, I don't train at all. I might exercise in my hotel room. But that's just because I am totally bored.

I am still amazed that I am around so many film and TV celebrities. Two of my good friends are Ben Vereen and Tony Orlando, for example. And I almost fainted one day when Charlton Heston called me and said he wanted to play tennis.

I sometimes play tennis with Steve Garvey, the Los Angeles Dodgers' first-baseman. You have seen his huge forearms. You would think that, with those arms, he would have a tough serve. But he is the same on the tennis court as he is on the baseball diamond—very controlled.

Now that I don't have to concentrate on the decathlon, I can even enter tennis tournaments.

Another of my favorite tennis partners—Desi Arnaz, Jr.

Never a hair out of place. He has a perfect tennis stroke. He never hits the ball terribly hard, but keeps putting it back until you miss it.

One of my favorite tennis partners is Parker Stevenson of the now-discontinued "Hardy Boys" TV series. Parker is a very intelligent person. Well educated, too—after all, he graduated from Princeton. But he is shy.

Even though he treats everyone in a gentlemanly fashion, he does avoid crowds. His fans tend to be young teen-agers and they sometimes lose control and overpower him. So many people think that he is aloof, when he is just cautious.

That brings up one bad part of being a celebrity. Sometimes people knock other people over just to get near a famous person. I know how Parker feels. Chrystie got knocked down and trampled once.

Being recognized in public makes you more cautious. Even going out to eat can be a problem. Chrystie and I are forced to eat at home a lot and that is frustrating for Chrystie. She loves to go to restaurants.

But we have to pick places where there is some privacy. Otherwise, people will interrupt your meal asking for autographs, telling you what they think of you, or just chatting. Meanwhile, the food gets cold.

We seldom eat out in Hollywood or Beverly Hills. That's where the stargazers look for personalities. When

This is not exactly dining in private, but what can you do? (Photo by Wagner International Photos, Inc.)

USA
935

we get to a restaurant, I always have to take a chair that faces the wall.

We do have time for our hobbies. Chrystie loves to cook. If it weren't for her cooking, I would become a junk-food addict. She plays the piano, has completely redecorated our house, and can she sew! She even made her own wedding dress.

I got my pilot's license last year and just bought a plane. I have a Kawasaki motorcycle that I use in motocross. I'm afraid to ride it on the highway. If I got hit by a car, the car wouldn't have a dent in it but I sure would. I also am into jet-skiing as well as snow and water-skiing.

And I have another toy—a Porsche Turbo Carrera. The Porsche is white with a brown trim. I always said, when I was driving my old Porsche 914, that if I won the Olympics, my treat for twelve years of training would be the nicest Porsche made.

I thought then that I wanted a gold Porsche, because of the medal. But you take what you can get—unless you want to wait six months.

The license plate number on the car is 8618. That doesn't sound like a special number, but it is. It was my final score in the decathlon that set the Olympics world record. It also gives me the advantage of being able to check into a motel, sign the guest register, and know almost automatically what my license number is.

But to tell you the truth, now that we have the baby, the Porsche is not the most practical car for us. So I'm thinking of selling it and getting a Jeep. I don't intend to make the deal as an even trade, however.

Chrystie seems to be wondering who put up that Olympic banner. (Photo by Anne Kerschner)

The fearless motorcyclist in action. But I stay off the highway.

That's the Porsche and that's the license number.

I'm now involved with so many things that it is like the decathlon all over again. I do sports broadcasting. I give lectures. I'm being thought of as a movie actor. I work for charity. I do a wide variety of things and I have always liked doing many things at the same time. I may, as time goes on, get more specialized, but right now I enjoy the variety.

Giving lectures is a lot of fun. (Photo by Quicksilver John Brunk. Courtesy *Skagit Valley Herald*)

I love to fish. And I guess I love to ham it up for the camera, too.

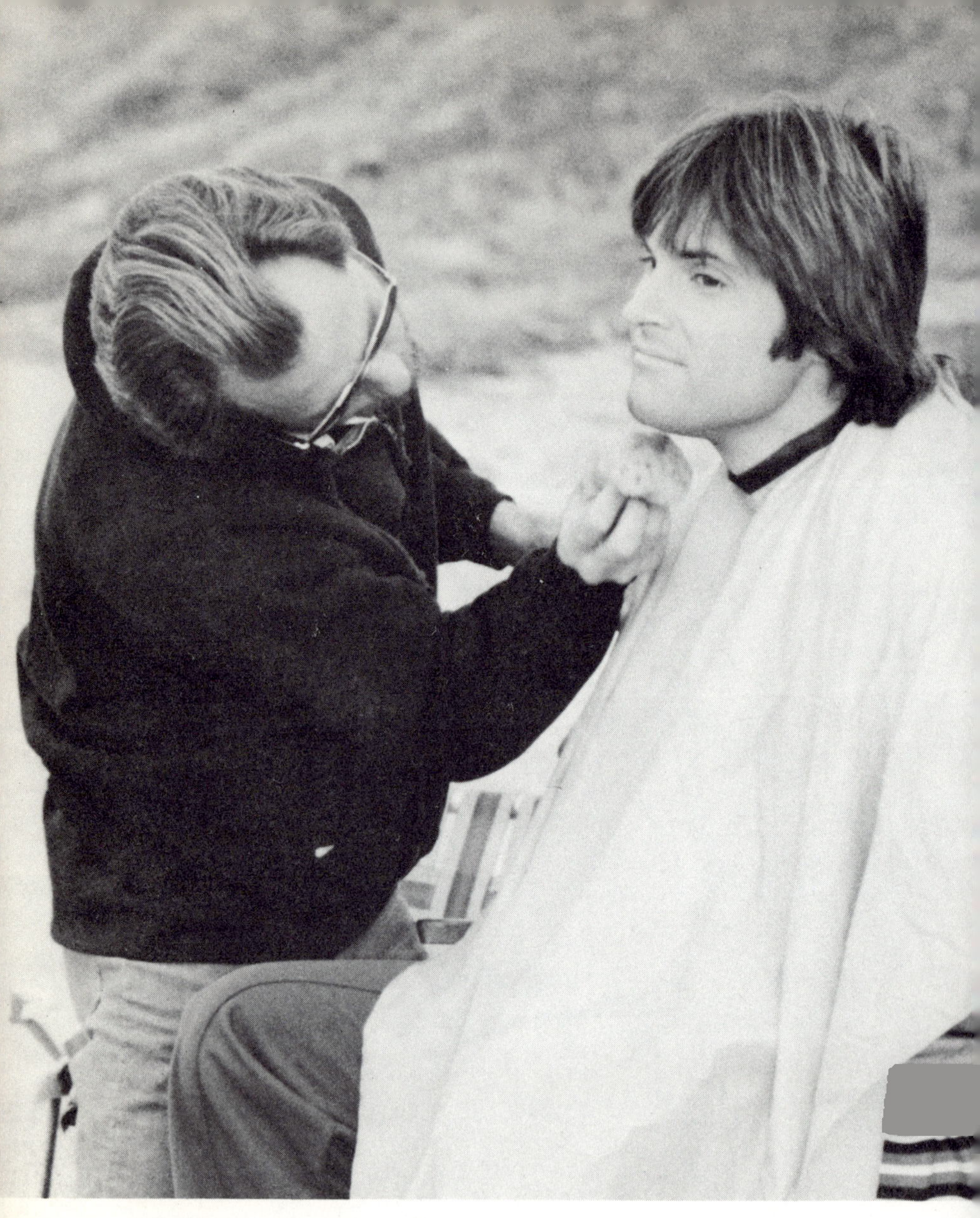

Getting ready for a commercial for the Bruce Jenner Running Shoe, made by the Brown Shoe Company. I still feel a little funny getting made up . . .

But now it's time to don the equipment. It looks as though my feet hurt a bit . . .

Finally, we're ready to roll the cameras. Here I am making sure that that log stays put.

I have had a lot of fun doing television commercials. Especially those Wheaties ads. By the way, I really do eat them almost every day.

Those Wheaties shooting sessions can be exhausting, though. Sometimes a one-minute commercial will take all day to shoot. You can follow to the last detail exactly what the director specified and he'll still reshoot over and over again. He sometimes seems to want it done a thousand different ways. Put your voice accent on this word. Take the accent off that word. Put the bananas on the cereal. Take the bananas off the cereal. And then there are other reasons for doing a take again. I sometimes spill the Wheaties on the table.

One thing I am really looking forward to is the 1980 Summer Olympics. These will be held in Moscow, and I will be one of three hosts for the National Broadcasting Company. The other two will be O. J. Simpson and Dick Enberg. We will be covering 150 hours of programing in sixteen days. We will be on the air all day long, it would seem.

Sometimes I will be explaining what is going on. Sometimes I will be tying in one event and going on to the next. NBC will have other experts around to help the three of us. For example, Frank Shorter, the 1972

With the great O.J. You know him for football, of course. And for running through airports. But did you know that he was also a track star at USC? That's why he will be on the Olympic telecasts. (Photo by Russell Turiak)

Olympics marathon winner, will be the expert on the distance events. And I will be, in addition to an anchor man, the expert on track and field events.

Who knows? I may be telling the audience all about some athlete who beats my decathlon world record.

If someone does, I will think it is great. I'd like to keep the record for a long time, but I hope I will have a good mental attitude about losing it. I hope I can say that "records are made to be broken." I hope I can feel that the man who beats me deserves what he has earned.

Whatever happens, my favorite color will still be gold.

7. Something Special

I have always been an admirer of people who work so hard that they become the best in the world at what they do. That means people like Ben Vereen, Vladimir Horowitz, Albert Einstein, and Pete Rose.

But there is another type of person that really commands my respect. That's the person who is not the best at what he or she does, but tries mightily to perform to the best of his or her abilities. That's why I am so involved in the Special Olympics for retarded children.

Those kids really turn me on. They try so hard. They give one hundred per cent and they are so pure about it. They are all winners. For them to participate at all takes a lot of guts. But they do more than just participate. They put everything they have into the Games.

Maybe I feel that way because I once had a problem of my own. When I was younger I did poorly in school. In the first and second grade I didn't even want to go to school. I was rebellious and refused to study. Even today I think that I'm not as good at the basic skills, such as reading and writing, as I might be.

Another one of my favorite achievers, Senator S. I. Hayakawa (R, California). He is one of the most famous semanticists in the world. In 1969 he was appointed president of San Francisco State University. And then, in 1976, three years after he had been retired, he was elected as a United States senator for the state of California.

It turned out that I had dyslexia. This is defined as a learning disability that slows your ability to read. Sometimes you see letters and words backward.

At that time, doctors did not diagnose dyslexia as well as they do now, so it took a while to find out I had it. Even today, I need a lot of practice beforehand if I'm called upon to read lines on television. I'm a good memorizer, but as far as picking things off a piece of paper cold goes, I can't do it very well.

So my heart goes out to anyone with a disability. And when the disabled person tries as hard as those kids in the Special Olympics do, I am so full of admiration that I want to tell the world about it. Think of a bunch of retarded kids running a race. Think of a brain-damaged child doing the long jump. I sometimes think that anyone who goes to see the Special Olympics and doesn't cry his eyes out is not human. I have so much respect for those kids.

That's why it's an honor to work with the Special Olympics. My good friend Rafer Johnson, is cochairman of the Athletes, Sportswriters, and Sportscasters for Special Olympics. It's a pleasure to work with him. And it's satisfying to see other personalities, from the sports or entertainment world, giving of their time to help—Sally Struthers, Mark Spitz, Susan Saint James, Cheryl Tiegs, Carol Channing, Frank Gifford, and Howard Cosell, to name only a few.

I am the national head coach for the track and field events, and what a group of coaches we have on the national staff. Bill Toomey, another Olympic decathlon

What a wonderful experience it is to participate in the Special Olympics. Look at the expressions on the faces of these three young athletes. And how wonderful are the people who give of their time to help put the show on the road. There is Carol Channing on the left and Eunice Kennedy Shriver on the right. Mrs. Shriver is the president of the Special Olympics. (Photo by Wagner International Photos, Inc.)

champion, is on the national coaching staff. From the world of boxing there are Muhammad Ali and George Foreman. Many football players are coaches: Buck Buchanan (Kansas City Chiefs), Rosie Grier (Los Angeles Rams), Lenny Moore (Baltimore Colts), Ray Schoenke

(Washington Redskins), Jan Stenerud (Kansas City Chiefs), and the former quarterback of the Dallas Cowboys, now a TV star, Don Meredith.

We have basketball players: Dave Cowens (Boston Celtics), Wayne Embry (Milwaukee Bucks), Keith Erickson (Los Angeles Lakers), Julius Erving (Philadelphia 76ers), and John Havlicek (Boston Celtics). Then there are the ice hocky players: Ken Hodge (Boston Bruins), Ed Westfall (New York Islanders), and Stan Mikita (Chicago Blackhawks). From baseball we have Carl Erskine (Los Angeles Dodgers) and Brooks Robinson (Baltimore Orioles).

To round the whole thing off, there are Suzy Chaffee, the Olympic skier; Gary Erwin, the world trampoline champion; Kyle Rote, Jr., the soccer star; and Keena Rothhammer, the Olympic swimmer. What a cast of coaches!

At last count, thirty-three countries have Special Olympic programs, and there are fifty state programs in the United States, plus programs in the District of Columbia, American Samoa, Guam, Puerto Rico, and the Virgin Islands. There are fourteen official Special Olympic sports: track and field, swimming, diving, gymnastics, floor hockey, basketball, ice skating, bowling, volleyball, poly hockey, Frisbee-disc, wheelchair events, soccer, and Alpine and Nordic skiing.

The Special Olympics is in fact an international program of physical fitness, sports training, and athletic competition for mentally retarded children and adults. No matter what a person's handicaps are, he or she can participate, because the athletes are grouped according

An arrival scene from a Special Olympics meet in Greenwich, Connecticut, in 1978. This is the beginning of an experience which will be a lasting memory for the Olympians, volunteers, coaches, parents, and friends. (Photo by Tony Minotti, Greenwich High School, Greenwich, Connecticut)

to ability. Someone in the least able group can still advance all the way to the International Games. All the athletes have to be is eight years of age or older.

There are about 10,000 local meets held every year. Then there are the State and National Games in which more than 100,000 athletes compete in the United States, and about 15,000 in various other countries.

International Games are held every four years. In

Dining at a restaurant with other Olympians is a sharing of a social experience. Here we see just a few of the athletes at the opening banquet in Greenwich. (Photo by Tony Minotti, Greenwich High School, Greenwich, Connecticut.)

the last one, held in 1979 at the State University of New York at Brockport, more than 3,500 competitors showed up from the United States and more than twenty other countries.

Let me describe how a typical Special Olympics Meet is run.

All of the athletes are expected to arrive at the Olympic Village on the day before the games start. This Olympic Village may be a hotel, a motel, a college

Before the parade starts, the athletes are grouped. (Photo by Tony Minotti, Greenwich High School, Greenwich, Connecticut)

dormitory, a military barracks, or even private houses in a residential area. Once the contestants get there, they are given their name tags and badges that say they are participating athletes.

Next, they are shown their rooms and they meet their roommates. It is now probably time for dinner. This may be a welcoming banquet.

Then the parade begins. Olympians throughout the world cherish that moment when they first entered the stadium for the opening ceremonies. (Photo by Tony Minotti, Greenwich High School, Greenwich, Connecticut)

Often a dance is held after dinner. Or there may be a movie or some sort of a stage performance. The athletes feel more relaxed after the festivities start. And we all know about all work and no play. The point of all this is to make the Olympics fun, not only hard work. And it is important that these kids get to know each other.

With the raising of the flag and the lighting of the torch, the Games begin. (Photo by Tony Minotti, Greenwich High School, Greenwich, Connecticut)

The next morning, the participants put on their uniforms and go to breakfast. After that, they go to the sports area.

Now it's time for the parade, just as in the other Olympic Games. The band starts up, and the kids, grouped together according to what school, city or county they come from, march past the reviewing

They're off! The Special Olympic events give the athletes an opportunity to compete, gain confidence, learn self-mastery, and improve in physical development. (Photo by Tony Minotti, Greenwich High School, Greenwich, Connecticut)

stand, carrying their banners. On the reviewing stand there may be members of the Kennedy family or representatives from Special Olympics, Inc. (The Kennedys have a special interest in the handicapped since one of the late President Kennedy's sisters is mentally retarded.) Special Olympics, Inc., whose president is Eunice Kennedy Shriver, and the Joseph P. Kennedy, Jr.,

Foundation are the sponsors of the Special Olympics. Also on the stand may be mayors, the state governor, sports stars, and show-business personalities, along with the athletes' families.

When the parade is over and all the athletes are standing in the center of the stadium, the American flag is raised. The Star-Spangled Banner is played.

Then in comes the runner carrying the Special Olympics torch. The Flame of Hope is lit from the torch, and the Special Olympics flag, whose colors are blue and gold, is raised.

A few short speeches are made. And then everyone recites the oath of the Special Olympics: "Let me win, but if I cannot win, let me be brave in the attempt."

It is time for the events to begin. You won't see all of the regular Olympic events here. But you will see some events that are not in the regular Olympics. The most common of these events are softball throwing, Frisbee throwing, and bowling.

In each event, everybody wins. People known as "huggers," are assigned everywhere. Every kid is hugged by a different person at the finish line. It doesn't matter whether the youngster came in first or last, somebody hugs him or her and says something like, "What a great job!" For many of those kids, just *finishing* is a triumph in itself.

Final instructions are given, as is a touch of encouragement. (Photo by Tony Minotti, Greenwich High School, Greenwich, Connecticut)

The thrill of victory. Take a look at that expression. (Photo by Tony Minotti, Greenwich High School, Greenwich, Connecticut)

Getting high on love. After every event is over, there is a "hugger" waiting for every participant. (Photo by Tony Minotti, Greenwich High School, Greenwich, Connecticut)

The first, second, and third place winners are given medals while standing on platforms just like those of the regular Olympics. Their names and their times or distances are announced. But everyone who participates gets a certificate.

Clinics are offered between the events on such subjects as physical fitness, basketball, trampoline, etc. These are often conducted by sports stars to teach some basic skills to the athletes.

In the middle of the day, the youngsters get a box lunch and have a sort of picnic.

After the afternoon events, tired and happy, the athletes go back to the Olympic Village. Since in some way everyone has been a winner, they are all ready for the victory banquet.

The next day, there are more events and clinics. Then there is the final parade. The Flame of Hope is extinguished till the next state meet, the flags are lowered, and everyone sings "Auld Lang Syne."

Who could fail to be moved? Who could fail to appreciate what these games do for the mental attitude of those retarded kids? Who could fail to be eager to help in the Special Olympics?

The Special Olympics is a volunteer program. More than 250,000 volunteers provide the manpower in the United States alone. These people come from high

Can you imagine how great it must feel to get a medal? (Photo by Tony Minotti, Greenwich High School, Greenwich, Connecticut)

A young athlete at the cycling clinic. Cycling is one of fifty separate activities in the fourteen sports areas which are available to the Special Olympics athletes. The scope of the clinic program is very broad, ranging from individual activities in cooking and baking to team sports under the supervision of celebrity athletes or college and high school coaches. In the unusual event being practiced for here, the bicyclist has to stay in the lane. It's like a two-wheel slalom. (Photo by Tony Minotti, Greenwich High School, Greenwich, Connecticut)

The event's over. There's the medal. And that's the coach's handshake. The reward of happiness for the coach is not the medal, but the happiness expressed by the Olympian. (Photo by Tony Minotti, Greenwich High School, Greenwich, Connecticut)

schools and colleges, service and women's clubs, parent groups, youth agencies; some are participants in and coaching sports; some are members of organizations and professional groups in education, special education, physical education, and recreation. Some other groups that help are the Office Education Association, the Jaycees, the Non-Commissioned Officers Association, and the American Legion.

But many more people are still needed. You may want to be one of the volunteers. Can you serve as a coach, a chaperone, a guide, a hugger, an organizer, a publicist, a fund raiser, a parade marshal, an entertainer, or a field official? Can you provide sports facilities, sports equipment, transportation, lodging, or meals? Can you contribute money? All these things are necessary if the Special Olympics are to remain successful.

And what do you get out of volunteering? Happiness and a sense of having helped someone. I remember how I felt when I was named to be the recipient of the 1978 Special Olympics Award for being the Outstanding International Sportscaster.

The citation read: "As Special Olympics Head Coach for Track and Field, Bruce Jenner has attended Games, bestowed medals and ribbons, helped with coaching and training, attended workshops and inspired families to play and grow together. In addition, he has covered Special Olympics events for ABC and has identified his leadership role in Special Olympics with his career as sportscaster and corporate spokesman."

I could not have been more proud.

8. Training

So you want to be a decathlete. Some of the things that I am going to say may strike you as silly. But I mean them.

To begin with, one of the best ways to start learning about the decathlon and how to run it is to go to the library. That may sound strange, but I don't know of a better way. Read books to get in your mind what you have to do. That is, read books to equip your mind about what your body has to do.

Suppose you are in junior high school. If you read all about the events in the decathlon and how to run them, there is a chance that you will know more about the decathlon than the coach. Of course, eventually you will need a coach. But remember that my best coach was Bertha, my dog.

I didn't have much coaching. Actually, I found that one of the best ways to improve decathlon techniques is to talk to people. My reasoning was that once I had found out what I wanted to be and what I wanted to do, I had to associate with those who had already done it. I would ask questions of them and profit from their experiences. By the way, this works in a lot of fields other than sports.

I also learned that I had to profit from my own experiences. After something good had happened, I sat down and asked myself why it happened that way. Too many people never sit down and think about why they won. They don't profit from the experience of winning. But the same people, when they lose, will sit down and think about why they lost. That's negative.

I say, do it both ways. Ask yourself, "Why did I do well?" as often as you ask yourself, "Why did I do badly?"

My attitude was always that I was in the decathlon for personal satisfaction. I was trying to see how good I could get. So after I ran my first decathlon, I sat down and said to myself, "Boy, I know you can improve a little bit here and there." It was me against the scorecard.

I did a television show recently with a group of mountain climbers and I think that they had something of the same attitude. It was just them against a mountain. But, on the other hand, these climbers work as a team. Decathletes are alone.

In preparing for the Olympics, I trained, on an average, six to eight hours a day. Every day. All year round. It was a full-time job.

I would get up about eight or nine in the morning and run. You hear about athletes who get up at the crack of dawn, but not this kid. I might run 5 miles,

I ran and ran. And then ran some more. (Photo by Chrystie Jenner)

and then I would be finished with my workout for a while. It would now be about ten A.M. I had already done my stretching and limbering-up exercises.

Next, I would practice this or that event until about one in the afternoon. After lunch, I would go on to my technique work for a couple of hours: putting the shot, pole-vaulting, and so on. Then I would do my hard running for a couple of more hours. Finally, I would lift weights. I would usually quit at about seven in the evening.

Every day was the same. I never managed to throw a discus or a javelin through anyone's window, although I almost hit a car once with a discus. I lost my grip on it and it slipped out of my hand.

I say that every day was the same, but what I mean is that I spent the same amount of time training each day. One nice thing about the decathlon is that if I didn't feel like putting the shot on a given day, there were nine other things I could practice.

There is a problem unique to decathlon training. I never believed that any one event was hard to train for, but there is a question of training for the whole. How do you practice being very fast in the 100-meter run and yet train to be fast in the 1,500-meter run too? The technique and strategy of these two runs are completely different. You have to train differently for each. That's why you never see any world-class sprinters who are also world-class distance runners.

I don't think that I was ever bored in training. I always loved it because I could see my future in it. There was my long-range goal. It was almost as if I were a gladiator, ready to challenge all the other athletes of the world. That made it fun and exciting, not boring.

Of course there is pain connected to training, but not in the sense of it being something awful. If the pain were awful, I never would have been an athlete. The pain is not like the pain of a broken arm. It's more like the pain of tiredness.

Yet that pain told me that I was getting closer to what I wanted to accomplish. That meant that it made me feel good.

Here is an example. Once a week I used to go out to a hill. It was about 300 meters to the top, and it was really steep. I would run up the hill, then run back down the hill. I did this twenty times, and it would take me about an hour. Every time I got to the top of the hill, I felt almost dead. But I would run back down and go right back up. Even with all that pain, I felt good, because I was getting closer to what I wanted to achieve.

Before we get to some of the specifics of training, there are a few general things to consider. First of all, training can be dangerous if you don't have the proper equipment. Doing the "Fosbury flop" over the bar in the high jump can hurt a lot if you don't have the proper padding to fall on. You are landing on your back.

Shoes are important, too. They should have good arch supports and soft soles, if you are going to run in them. A lot of shin splints can be prevented if you wear decent shoes. And be sure you have different shoes for the different events.

Warm up properly before you try anything. Work up a good sweat. Don't do anything until you feel limber. Your muscles should feel fairly fluid when you run. Your pulse rate should be high and you should have stretched your body out. You will learn to know when you have warmed up properly.

You must also be careful not to overextend yourself. Don't keep on going when you are too tired and worn out.

There is one thing that you won't have to practice. At least, I never had to. I refer to making faces. I make faces because I am trying so hard. I also have to grunt and groan and yell and scream. When you are putting out one hundred per cent, sometimes that one hundred per cent will show in your face.

Now let's get down to specifics. The decathlon breaks down into two areas—strength and speed. There is really only one endurance event, the 1,500-meter run.

You have to have speed for the runs and the hurdles, for the approach to the long jump, and so on. You have to have strength to throw the javelin or put the shot, or even to run the hurdles and the 1,500. Let's suppose you have the strength and speed; now it's time to develop your techniques.

The first event is the 100-meter run, and it is really a sprint. The technique of sprinting is mostly having a good reaction time off the blocks. There is more arm movement and higher leg lift in the sprints. You are running flat out as fast as you can.

There is no such thing as pacing in the 100-meter run. I used to think of the sprint lane as a railroad track. I wanted to accelerate as fast as I could to get to my top speed and then hold that speed to the tape.

But back to the speed off the blocks. I used to try to anticipate the starting gun—that way, I would be one step out when the gun went off. But more and more meets are being timed electronically, as were the 1976 Olympics, and you can't beat the pistol. The gun is wired to a sensing device as are the starting blocks under your feet. If you take your foot off the block before the gun goes off, the sensor knows it, and you are charged with a false start.

As far as your morale in the decathlon is concerned, the 100-meter may be the most important event, because it is the first event. If someone beats you by a mere 2/10 second, he is already more than 50 points ahead of you. That can be scary. You have put out so much in less than 11 seconds, and already you are behind.

When I was running, here is the way I attacked the 100-meter run. As I said, if I weren't being timed electronically, I would try to jump the gun the first time. I wanted to be in the act of moving when the gun went off. You are allowed two false starts in the 100-meter, so there was no harm done if I jumped off too fast the first time. And beating the gun may mean a difference of 1/10 of a second on your time.

The first 60 meters are spent on acceleration, trying to hit your top speed. The next 30 meters you concentrate on maintaining that speed. The last 10 meters should be given over to a final spurt—that's the hard part, but it is essential.

In the long jump, I use an approach of 118 feet. That approach run is shorter than most jumpers use, but it seems to suit me. You will have to find your own ideal distance. I take the same number of steps every time. I don't know how many steps I take, but it is always the same number. Again, you will have to find your own ideal number.

I run as fast as I can, and the last time my left foot comes down—this will be on the ramp—I put it down flat-footed. I keep my center of gravity as low as possible. Then my right foot hits the ramp and pushes my left leg up, and I am airborne.

WARNING: When I talk about using left and right feet, left and right legs, or left arms and right arms, don't take me too literally. You may want to reverse these techniques. Remember that I am left-handed.

I start out the shot put standing at the rear of the circle with my back toward where I will be putting the shot. Holding the shot in my left hand, I tuck it right up by my left ear. My body turns halfway around as I swing my right foot, which is my front foot, ahead of my body. I keep my weight low so that as much of the mass of my body is behind the shot as possible. Then I push the shot, trying to get drive with my legs. This push with the arm should be made as quickly and strongly as possible. Flick the shot with your wrist at the last moment.

I'm just about ready to push the shot away. Notice that my left leg muscles are tightened, ready to give me extra leverage.

When I first started doing the high jump, I straddled or rolled over the bar. Then Dick Fosbury invented the Fosbury flop. He went over the bar backward with his head and shoulders first and found that the rest of his body naturally followed. I've been doing that flop since 1971.

I use an 11-step approach to the bar, but not a straight 11-step run. I take the run in the form of the letter J. The first 6 steps, starting off to the left end of the bar, are straight. But then I cut on my left foot and take the last 5 steps in a curving path toward the bar. My right leg is planted and my left knee is brought up almost to my chest. My whole body goes up in the air, with my back to the bar. I concentrate on getting my hips over the bar, then bringing up my legs.

The 400-meter run is a dash or sprint, but it is a long one. I try to get up my momentum as soon as possible. The last 100 meters will be murder—you are exhausted and you are only three quarters of the way to the tape. The 400-meter is so long that you have curves in the course, and that makes you slow down. But the main point is for you to maintain maximum speed throughout the run.

If you are actually participating in a decathlon, these five events mark the end of the first day of competition. But you can't quit now. You have built up a lot of lactic acid in your muscles. If you don't get rid of it, you will have cramps and sore muscles the next morning. After the 400-meter, jog a mile. Your blood will redistribute that lactic acid in your body.

My body has twisted in the air and I am throwing the pole away.

The 110-meter hurdles are also a sprint. You just have to go as fast as you can. There are ten hurdles, 10 meters apart. The trick is to take only 3 steps in between each two hurdles. If you don't keep up your speed, the 3 steps may increase to 4 or 5. That will mess up your time.

As in the shot put, I start out the discus throw with my back toward where I want to throw. I turn around, quickly and explosively, one and one half times, and then let go. More than in any other event, the wind can hurt you in the discus. It may make a difference of up to 5 meters, so try to keep your throw from being too high.

In the pole vault, I use an approach of 131 feet. You will have to experiment to find out how long your approach should be. Two strides away from the pit, I raise one end of the pole and put the other end in the planting box. I'm at full speed at this point. The pole bends and I am airborne. I swing my legs up over my head. At this point I am upside down. My legs go over the bar and my body twists so that I can throw the pole away.

The javelin is a spear. But you don't really throw it. You run, then plant your feet, and then *pull* the javelin over your shoulder. The motion is started with your weight on the back foot, and as you push the javelin, you shift your weight to the front foot.

For me, the event that requires the most work is the 1,500-meter run. A lot of your success in it will depend on your conditioning, guts, and desire. I look

And, oh, the thrill of landing after a successful pole vault, especially in the Olympics! (*Sports Illustrated* Photo)

upon the 1,500-meter as being a run with four segments. There are three segments of 400 meters each, which I try to run in 75 seconds each. Then there is the final segment of 300 meters, which I try to run in 45 seconds. That means I really speed up on the last segment.

You also have to worry about pace and strategy in the 1,500-meter run. You have to think who the other athletes are in the race and what their pace will be. You have to ask yourself, "Is their pace going to throw me off?" If one of them is running faster than you, you might have a tendency to speed up yourself. This may destroy your strategy. You must learn to know your own pace and keep to it no matter what the other runners do. I used to know exactly what my pace was. I could go out on the track and run 68-second laps without even being timed.

Now let's say that you are really serious about becoming a decathlete. Here is some advice. To begin with, I strongly recommend that if you are interested in the decathlon, you join the Decathlon Association (DECA). It is an organization of those who enjoy and support the decathlon: athletes, former athletes, coaches, meet directors, and fans. DECA was formed in 1974, and its main activity so far has been the publishing of informational materials. It has published *The Decathlon Book* and *The Decathlon Guide*, as well as occasional newsletters.

To join DECA, send your name, permanent address, and $3.00 (make checks or money orders payable to DECA) for dues to the acting treasurer:

Here I am about to shift my weight to the front foot in order to push off the javelin better.

Frank Zarnowski
Faculty
Mount St. Mary's College
Emmitsburg, Maryland 21727

Frank Zarnowski is an expert in his field and a reliable source of information and assistance.

Now for the training schedule.

In the fall, run long distances in the morning and in the afternoon, working up to a point where you can run 5 miles each time. Twice a week, do hill work. A deserted golf course is a good place. Don't do much track work during this season, because you are trying to build yourself up, not trying to better your techniques. Practicing throwing the javelin might be a good idea, however.

In the winter, move onto the track and begin doing some interval-type workouts. These are mostly long distances like the 880, the 660, the 440, and the 330, where you jog between each run. Keep up the hill work and try to increase both the speed and the load of the workout. Begin some jumping, and gradually work into free runs in each event.

In the spring, discontinue the hill work and begin to do quality workouts—for the 500, the 440, the 330, and 220, with a walk in between. As you approach your first competition, begin to do four 220s and three 330s at race pace or better. Practice pole vaulting and hurdling, as well as working on the long-jump and high-jump runs without actually jumping.

The summer is the peak competition season, of course. Do only quality workouts: three 220s, two 330s, or 325, 220, and 165. Sometimes do three 100-meter runs for time with a running start. Work on technique in the throws. Vault and hurdle a lot.

Weight-lifting is important, too. Try to get as strong as you possibly can. Work on lifting your upper body one day, your lower body the next day, and then rest a day. On the days you lift, lift very heavy weights.

Lifting the upper body should consist of all of the following:

Sit-ups using a weight behind the head.
Dumbbell presses on an inclined bench (start at 50 pounds and work up to 110 pounds).
Jerks taking the bar off the rack (five sets with five repeats).
Pullovers (four sets repeated ten times).

Lifting the lower body should consist of all of the following:

Squats (five sets repeated five times, carrying as much weight as possible)
Hamstring curls (four sets of ten repeats)
Toe rises (four sets of ten repeats)

Then there is sequence training. I usually didn't use sequence training because I seemed to know what events I felt like doing each particular day. It all depends on how you feel, both physically and mentally.

Even with all that training, however, I always believed that all work and no play would make Bruce a dull boy.

However, my workouts always consisted of the following:

Mile jog
Stretching
Four 100-meter runs on grass
More stretching
Two 100-meter runs on the track
One or more throwing events
One or two 110-meter runs
Interval running

And since you are going to enter a jumping event, practice it.

I often get letters telling me about the writer's own individual training programs. One thing that seems to me to be common to most of these letters is the lack of emphasis on training for the 1,500-meter run. I cannot stress enough the importance of developing your performance in this event. It is next to impossible to win the decathlon if you neglect the 1,500-meter. In fact, some decathletes have been referred to as "classic nine-eventers." They have worked on perfecting the first nine events, ignoring the tenth.

Most importantly, you must be dedicated, working every day—not just once or twice a week. If you don't enjoy what you are doing or if you are procrastinating about training, face the fact that the decathlon is not for you. Go on to something more productive and fulfilling. The decathlon is becoming more and more competitive each year. You must work every day if you hope to achieve your goals. I trained for twelve years; no one can hope to be an overnight success.

9. Some Final Thoughts

It seems to me that most people want to have a hero. And, because of what I did in the Olympics, some of them consider me to be a hero. I know that sounds egotistical, but it happens to be true: some people do.

I might not be their hero if they knew me personally, because I am as human as everyone else. But they look upon my image as being something to admire. So I try to keep that image untarnished.

I try to be careful of what I say and do, because I have a responsibility to the people who look up to me. I'm not trying to act the "All-American boy" who eats nothing but apple pie and ice cream, but I know that a lot of the things that I say and do have an influence on others, especially kids.

Heroes have changed. When I was a kid, we used to have war heroes. Today, most of the kid's heroes are athletes. My own heroes are people who are good in any area. I don't care if it's music, business, entertainment, or sports—just people who are the best at what they do. I respect people who, like me, say to themselves, "I'm not going to do something unless I can be good at it."

I want kids to respect me, and I hope I'll never let them down. (Photo by R. Smith Kiliper)

How do you get to be like that? I don't know how you get to be a skilled astronaut, a great writer, or a fine comedian, but I can give some advice on becoming a good athlete. First of all, don't go into sports thinking that you are going to make a million dollars from it. There are very few people able to do that. You read about huge sums being paid to professional athletes, but take a look at what some of the other members of the team are making. They may get much smaller salaries, stay on the team for only five or six years, and then end up with almost nothing.

Lay out realistic goals for yourself, and then take it one step at a time. Suppose you want to play professional basketball. First try to make your junior high school team. If that happens, great. You have done something with your talent. Then, if you are good in junior high school, you can say to yourself, "Maybe I can make the high school team."

So you play on the high school team. Then you start thinking that you might be good enough to get a college basketball scholarship. If you are a college star, you might get a pro contract. Those are the steps along the way, and you have to take them one at a time.

But life is not all sports. It has its intellectual side, and that is every bit as important as the physical side.

If you look carefully at the people who are good at sports, you will be surprised at how many of them are, or were, good academically. When I got into sports I soon learned that to remain eligible, I had to make certain grades. I also found out that the better I did in my school work, the better I was doing on the athletic field. Life seemed to go easier. If I were worried about school, passing tests, or being promoted, I couldn't concentrate on sports.

There is another reason to do well in school. Being heavily involved in sports on a competitive level takes up perhaps only ten years of your life. But what you learn in class stays with you forever. The only way to be sure that you will make a success out of your life is to do well in school.

School teaches you the basics of mental self-discipline. And even sports have become more mental than they used to be. Football players, for example, have to be much smarter than they were years ago—have you seen a professional football playbook lately?

What I have just said goes for women, too. Up until about ten years ago, women were not totally accepted in sports. It was said that sports made women huge, strong, and masculine. That's nonsense.

Fortunately, women today are realizing what they can do in sports. And they have become respected. Whether it is in track and field, gymnastics, tennis, or almost any other sport, women are really coming on now. And I think that's great.

There is even a decathlon-type event for women—the pentathlon. It is a series of five events—the long jump, the low hurdles, the half-mile run, the high jump, and the shot put.

We don't hear about it much in this country, but it is an Olympic event. Probably the reason for it being little known here is because we have never had a champion in the pentathlon. At the 1976 Montreal Olym-

Chrystie has always been by my side. (Photo by Anne Kerschner)

pics, the first-, second-, and third-place medals went to three East German women. Since Americans always seem to want to see an American win at the Olympics, the women's pentathlon never seems to get any TV time. It's something like field hockey. Played by men at the Olympics, field hockey is a fantastic sport. But in the United States we think of it as being played exclusively by women. And it never gets on television.

People have asked me what I would do if I were in charge of the Olympics. Before I answer, let me tell you about the Olympics.

In the United States, if you want to prepare for the Olympics, you have to do it on your own, financially. If you have a working wife, as I did, you may be able to train enough to be successful. I cannot tell you how lucky I was to have Chrystie for a wife. She supported me both financially and emotionally. That meant I had time and incentive to train.

Otherwise, you have to be either wealthy or fortunate enough to have a very understanding boss. I know of American world-record holders who have to live off food stamps in order to train. I've always said that there must be a better way.

We have the best coaches in the world. They are coaches whose methods are copied by the rest of the world. Our system of education—elementary school, junior high, high school, and college—is tailor-made for the development of young athletes. American kids spend more years in school, on the average, than the kids of almost any other country in the world.

But after college, the competitive athlete has to face a cruel world. He has lost his coach and is on his own financially. This is not true in many other countries, where the athletes out of school are subsidized by the state.

Now here's my plan. I'd get American business and industry to sponsor training centers for American amateur athletes. These centers should have dormitories, gyms, medical facilities, stadiums, and lots and lots of equipment. Then I'd let the good athletes use the centers whenever they want.

Next, I'd eliminate the competition between the two ruling bodies of amateur sports, the National Collegiate Athletic Association and the Amateur Athletic Union. They always seem to be bickering with each other, and the athletes suffer. Perhaps they can be combined.

So there you have it. All I want is for the athletes of this country to have good places to train and for the people who run amateur sports to stop behaving like politicians. If this were to happen, there would be no limit to the successes possible for American athletes. Speaking for all of them, I say that there is nothing that they will not be able to do.

INDEX

798.4
JENNER
CF04 C1